50 American Morning Meal Recipes for Home

By: Kelly Johnson

Table of Contents

- Classic Pancakes
- French Toast
- tBlueberry Muffins
- Eggs Benedict
- Breakfast Burritos
- Buttermilk Waffles
- Breakfast Sandwiches
- Denver Omelette
- Cinnamon Rolls
- Banana Pancakes
- Huevos Rancheros
- Sausage Gravy and Biscuits
- Quiche Lorraine
- Breakfast Potatoes
- Corned Beef Hash
- Belgian Waffles
- Biscuits and Gravy
- Breakfast Tacos
- Oatmeal with Fruit
- Bagels with Lox
- Scrambled Eggs with Smoked Salmon
- Cinnamon French Toast
- Avocado Toast with Poached Eggs
- Breakfast Quesadillas
- Breakfast Pizza
- Hash Brown Casserole
- Veggie Frittata
- Pumpkin Pancakes
- Baked Oatmeal
- Breakfast Skillet
- Lemon Poppy Seed Muffins
- Greek Yogurt Parfait
- Breakfast Strata
- Apple Cinnamon Pancakes
- Monte Cristo Sandwich
- Cranberry Scones

- Breakfast Quinoa
- Cheddar Bacon Biscuits
- Smoked Salmon Bagel Sandwich
- Breakfast Enchiladas
- Spinach and Feta Quiche
- Nutella Stuffed French Toast
- Breakfast BLT
- Blueberry Breakfast Cake
- Breakfast Stuffed Peppers
- Peanut Butter Banana Smoothie
- Strawberry Shortcake Pancakes
- Southwest Breakfast Casserole
- Pecan Sticky Buns
- Chocolate Chip Pancakes

Classic Pancakes

Ingredients:

- 1 cup all-purpose flour
- 2 tablespoons granulated sugar
- 1 teaspoon baking powder
- 1/2 teaspoon baking soda
- 1/4 teaspoon salt
- 3/4 cup buttermilk (or substitute with 3/4 cup milk + 1 tablespoon vinegar or lemon juice)
- 1/4 cup milk
- 1 large egg
- 2 tablespoons unsalted butter, melted
- 1 teaspoon vanilla extract (optional)
- Butter or oil for cooking
- Maple syrup, fresh berries, or toppings of your choice

Instructions:

1. **Preheat Griddle or Pan:** Heat a griddle or large non-stick skillet over medium heat. You can test if it's hot enough by sprinkling a few drops of water on it - if they sizzle and evaporate, it's ready.
2. **Prepare Dry Ingredients:** In a large bowl, whisk together the flour, sugar, baking powder, baking soda, and salt.
3. **Prepare Wet Ingredients:** In another bowl, whisk together the buttermilk, milk, egg, melted butter, and vanilla extract (if using).
4. **Combine:** Pour the wet ingredients into the dry ingredients and gently mix until just combined. It's okay if there are some lumps in the batter; overmixing can make the pancakes tough.
5. **Cook Pancakes:** Add a little butter or oil to the griddle or skillet and swirl to coat. Pour 1/4 cup of batter for each pancake onto the hot surface. Cook until bubbles form on the surface of the pancakes and the edges look set, about 2-3 minutes.
6. **Flip and Cook:** Carefully flip the pancakes with a spatula and cook until golden brown on the other side, about 1-2 minutes more.
7. **Serve:** Transfer the pancakes to a plate and keep warm in a low oven (if desired) while you cook the remaining pancakes. Serve warm with maple syrup, fresh berries, or your favorite toppings.

Enjoy your classic pancakes as a delightful breakfast treat!

French Toast

Ingredients:

- 4 slices of bread (thick slices like Texas toast or brioche work well)
- 2 large eggs

- 1/2 cup milk
- 1 tablespoon granulated sugar
- 1/2 teaspoon vanilla extract
- 1/4 teaspoon ground cinnamon (optional)
- Pinch of salt
- Butter or oil for cooking
- Maple syrup, powdered sugar, fresh berries, or toppings of your choice

Instructions:

1. **Prepare Bread:** If using thick slices of bread, you can leave them out on the counter for a few minutes to slightly dry out (this helps the bread absorb the egg mixture better).
2. **Make Egg Mixture:** In a shallow bowl or pie plate, whisk together the eggs, milk, sugar, vanilla extract, cinnamon (if using), and salt until well combined.
3. **Soak Bread:** Dip each slice of bread into the egg mixture, turning to coat both sides thoroughly. Let the bread soak in the mixture for about 20-30 seconds per side, allowing it to absorb the liquid but not become too soggy.
4. **Cook French Toast:** Heat a large skillet or griddle over medium heat and add a pat of butter or a drizzle of oil. Once the butter is melted and the skillet is hot, add the soaked bread slices in a single layer.
5. **Cook Until Golden:** Cook the French Toast for about 3-4 minutes on each side, or until golden brown and cooked through. Adjust the heat as needed to ensure the French Toast cooks evenly without burning.
6. **Serve:** Transfer the cooked French Toast to plates and serve warm with maple syrup, powdered sugar, fresh berries, or any other toppings you prefer.

Enjoy your homemade French Toast as a delightful breakfast treat!

Blueberry Muffins

Ingredients:

- 1 and 1/2 cups all-purpose flour
- 3/4 cup granulated sugar
- 1/2 teaspoon salt
- 2 teaspoons baking powder
- 1/3 cup vegetable oil or melted butter
- 1 large egg
- 1/3 - 1/2 cup milk (start with 1/3 cup and add more if needed)
- 1 and 1/2 teaspoons vanilla extract
- 1 cup fresh or frozen blueberries (if using frozen, do not thaw)

Instructions:

1. **Preheat Oven and Prepare Muffin Tin:** Preheat your oven to 375°F (190°C). Line a 12-cup muffin tin with paper liners or grease the cups with butter or cooking spray.
2. **Mix Dry Ingredients:** In a large bowl, whisk together the flour, sugar, salt, and baking powder until well combined.
3. **Prepare Wet Ingredients:** In a separate bowl, whisk together the vegetable oil (or melted butter), egg, milk, and vanilla extract until smooth.
4. **Combine Wet and Dry Ingredients:** Pour the wet ingredients into the dry ingredients and gently stir with a spatula or wooden spoon until just combined. Be careful not to overmix; a few lumps in the batter are okay.
5. **Fold in Blueberries:** Gently fold the blueberries into the batter. If using frozen blueberries, coat them lightly with flour before adding to the batter to prevent them from sinking to the bottom of the muffins.
6. **Fill Muffin Cups:** Divide the batter evenly among the prepared muffin cups, filling each about 2/3 full.
7. **Bake:** Bake the muffins in the preheated oven for 18-20 minutes, or until the tops are golden brown and a toothpick inserted into the center of a muffin comes out clean.
8. **Cool and Serve:** Allow the muffins to cool in the pan for 5 minutes, then transfer them to a wire rack to cool completely. Serve warm or at room temperature.

Enjoy your homemade blueberry muffins as a delightful addition to your breakfast or brunch!

Eggs Benedict

Ingredients:

- 4 large eggs
- 2 English muffins, split and toasted
- 4 slices Canadian bacon or ham
- 1 tablespoon white vinegar (for poaching eggs)
- Chopped fresh chives or parsley, for garnish (optional)

Hollandaise Sauce:

- 3 large egg yolks
- 1 tablespoon water
- 1 tablespoon lemon juice
- 1/2 cup (1 stick) unsalted butter, melted and hot
- Pinch of cayenne pepper (optional)
- Salt and pepper to taste

Instructions:

1. **Prepare Hollandaise Sauce:**
    - Fill a small saucepan with a couple of inches of water and bring to a simmer over medium heat.
    - In a heatproof bowl that fits snugly over the saucepan (but does not touch the water), whisk together the egg yolks, water, and lemon juice until smooth.
    - Place the bowl over the simmering water (double boiler method) and whisk constantly until the mixture begins to thicken, about 2-3 minutes. Be careful not to let the eggs scramble.
    - Slowly drizzle in the melted butter, whisking constantly, until the sauce is smooth and thickened. Season with cayenne pepper (if using), salt, and pepper. Remove from heat but keep the bowl over the warm water to keep the sauce warm while you prepare the rest of the dish.
2. **Poach Eggs:**
    - Fill a large, shallow saucepan with about 2 inches of water and add the vinegar. Bring the water to a simmer over medium heat.
    - Crack each egg into a small cup or ramekin. Gently slide each egg into the simmering water, one at a time. Poach for about 3-4 minutes, until the whites are set but the yolks are still runny.
    - Remove the poached eggs with a slotted spoon and drain on a paper towel-lined plate.
3. **Assemble Eggs Benedict:**
    - Place the toasted English muffin halves on serving plates. Top each half with a slice of Canadian bacon or ham.
    - Carefully place a poached egg on top of each muffin half.

4. **Serve:**
    - Spoon hollandaise sauce generously over each poached egg and sprinkle with chopped chives or parsley for garnish, if desired.
    - Serve immediately while warm.

Enjoy your homemade Eggs Benedict as a delicious and elegant breakfast or brunch dish!

Breakfast Burritos

Ingredients:

- 4 large eggs
- 1/4 cup milk
- Salt and pepper, to taste
- 1 tablespoon butter or oil
- 4 large flour tortillas
- 1 cup shredded cheese (cheddar, Monterey Jack, or a blend)
- 1 cup cooked breakfast sausage, bacon, or ham, chopped
- 1/2 cup diced bell peppers (any color)
- 1/4 cup diced onion
- 1/4 cup diced tomatoes
- Salsa, avocado slices, sour cream, or other toppings of your choice

Instructions:

1. **Cook the Eggs:**
   - In a bowl, whisk together the eggs, milk, salt, and pepper until well combined.
   - Heat butter or oil in a large skillet over medium heat. Pour in the egg mixture and cook, stirring occasionally, until the eggs are scrambled and just set. Remove from heat.
2. **Prepare the Fillings:**
   - In the same skillet (if it's large enough), add a little more oil if needed and sauté the diced bell peppers and onions until softened, about 3-4 minutes.
3. **Assemble the Burritos:**
   - Warm the flour tortillas briefly in the microwave or in a dry skillet for a few seconds to make them pliable.
   - Divide the scrambled eggs, shredded cheese, cooked breakfast meat, sautéed vegetables, and diced tomatoes evenly among the tortillas, placing the fillings in a line down the center of each tortilla.
4. **Fold the Burritos:**
   - Fold in the sides of each tortilla, then roll it up tightly from the bottom to enclose the fillings.
5. **Serve:**
   - If desired, you can heat the assembled burritos in a skillet over medium heat for a few minutes on each side to crisp up the tortilla and melt the cheese.
   - Serve the breakfast burritos immediately, optionally with salsa, avocado slices, sour cream, or your favorite toppings on the side.

Enjoy your homemade breakfast burritos as a filling and delicious morning meal! They can also be wrapped individually in foil and stored in the refrigerator for a few days or frozen for longer storage.

Buttermilk Waffles

Ingredients:

- 2 cups all-purpose flour
- 2 tablespoons granulated sugar
- 2 teaspoons baking powder
- 1 teaspoon baking soda
- 1/2 teaspoon salt
- 2 cups buttermilk
- 1/2 cup unsalted butter, melted and cooled slightly
- 2 large eggs
- 1 teaspoon vanilla extract

Instructions:

1. **Preheat Waffle Iron:**
   - Preheat your waffle iron according to manufacturer's instructions.
2. **Mix Dry Ingredients:**
   - In a large bowl, whisk together the flour, sugar, baking powder, baking soda, and salt.
3. **Mix Wet Ingredients:**
   - In another bowl, whisk together the buttermilk, melted butter, eggs, and vanilla extract until well combined.
4. **Combine Wet and Dry Ingredients:**
   - Pour the wet ingredients into the dry ingredients and stir until just combined. The batter may be slightly lumpy, but avoid overmixing.
5. **Cook Waffles:**
   - Lightly grease the waffle iron with non-stick cooking spray or brush with melted butter.
   - Pour enough batter onto the hot waffle iron to cover the grids (amount will depend on your waffle iron size).
   - Close the lid and cook according to the manufacturer's instructions, typically 3-5 minutes, or until the waffles are golden brown and crisp.
6. **Serve:**
   - Carefully remove the waffles from the iron and serve immediately while warm.
   - Repeat with the remaining batter, greasing the waffle iron as needed.
7. **Optional Toppings:**
   - Serve the buttermilk waffles with toppings such as maple syrup, fresh berries, whipped cream, powdered sugar, or any other toppings of your choice.

Enjoy your homemade buttermilk waffles as a delicious and satisfying breakfast!

Breakfast Sandwiches

Ingredients:

- 4 English muffins or sandwich buns
- 4 large eggs
- Salt and pepper, to taste
- 4 slices of cheese (cheddar, American, Swiss, etc.)
- 4 slices of cooked bacon or breakfast sausage patties
- Butter or oil for cooking

Optional Additions:

- Sliced tomatoes
- Avocado slices
- Spinach or arugula leaves
- Sliced ham or Canadian bacon
- Breakfast potatoes or hash browns

Instructions:

1. **Cook Eggs:**
   - Heat a non-stick skillet over medium heat and add a little butter or oil.
   - Crack the eggs into the skillet and season with salt and pepper. Cook the eggs to your desired doneness (scrambled, fried, or poached).
2. **Assemble Sandwiches:**
   - Toast the English muffins or sandwich buns lightly until golden brown.
   - Place a slice of cheese on the bottom half of each toasted muffin or bun.
   - Top each with a cooked egg (folded or whole, depending on preference).
   - Add a slice of cooked bacon or sausage patty on top of the egg.
3. **Optional Additions:**
   - Add any optional toppings like sliced tomatoes, avocado, spinach, ham, or breakfast potatoes.
4. **Serve:**
   - Top with the other half of the toasted muffin or bun to complete the sandwich.
   - Serve the breakfast sandwiches warm and enjoy!

Variations:

- **Vegetarian Option:** Skip the bacon or sausage and add extra veggies like sautéed mushrooms or bell peppers.
- **Croissant Sandwich:** Use croissants instead of English muffins for a flakier texture.
- **Wrap Variation:** Instead of using bread or muffins, wrap all the ingredients in a large tortilla for a breakfast burrito-style sandwich.

These breakfast sandwiches are customizable and perfect for a quick and satisfying morning meal. Enjoy experimenting with different ingredients and flavors!

Denver Omelette

Ingredients:

- 4 large eggs
- 1/4 cup milk
- Salt and pepper, to taste
- 1 tablespoon butter or oil
- 1/2 cup diced cooked ham
- 1/4 cup diced onion
- 1/4 cup diced bell peppers (any color)
- 1/2 cup shredded cheddar cheese (or cheese of your choice)
- Optional toppings: Salsa, avocado slices, sour cream, chopped chives or parsley

Instructions:

1. **Prepare Ingredients:**
   - In a bowl, whisk together the eggs, milk, salt, and pepper until well combined. Set aside.
2. **Cook Filling:**
   - In a large non-stick skillet, melt the butter or heat the oil over medium heat.
   - Add the diced ham, onion, and bell peppers to the skillet. Cook, stirring occasionally, until the vegetables are softened and the ham is lightly browned, about 3-4 minutes.
3. **Add Eggs:**
   - Pour the egg mixture evenly over the cooked ham and vegetables in the skillet.
4. **Cook the Omelette:**
   - As the eggs begin to set around the edges, gently push them towards the center of the skillet with a spatula. Tilt the skillet to let the uncooked eggs flow to the edges.
   - Continue cooking until the eggs are mostly set but still slightly runny on top.
5. **Add Cheese:**
   - Sprinkle the shredded cheese evenly over one half of the omelette.
6. **Fold and Serve:**
   - Using a spatula, carefully fold the omelette in half to cover the cheese.
   - Cook for another minute or until the cheese is melted and the eggs are fully cooked through.
7. **Serve:**
   - Slide the Denver omelette onto a serving plate. Garnish with optional toppings such as salsa, avocado slices, sour cream, or chopped chives or parsley.
   - Serve hot and enjoy your delicious Denver omelette!

This recipe makes one large Denver omelette, which you can customize with your favorite toppings and serve as a satisfying breakfast or brunch dish.

Cinnamon Rolls

Ingredients:

For the dough:

- 1 cup warm milk (around 110°F)
- 2 and 1/4 teaspoons active dry yeast (1 packet)
- 1/2 cup granulated sugar
- 1/3 cup unsalted butter, melted
- 2 large eggs
- 1 teaspoon salt
- 4 and 1/2 cups all-purpose flour

For the filling:

- 1 cup packed brown sugar
- 2 and 1/2 tablespoons ground cinnamon
- 1/3 cup unsalted butter, softened

For the cream cheese frosting:

- 4 ounces cream cheese, softened
- 1/4 cup unsalted butter, softened
- 1 cup powdered sugar
- 1/2 teaspoon vanilla extract
- Pinch of salt

Instructions:

1. **Activate Yeast:**
    - In a small bowl, combine warm milk, yeast, and 1 tablespoon of the granulated sugar. Let it sit for about 5-10 minutes until foamy.
2. **Make Dough:**
    - In a large mixing bowl or the bowl of a stand mixer fitted with a dough hook, combine the yeast mixture, melted butter, remaining sugar, eggs, salt, and 4 cups of flour. Mix until combined.
    - Gradually add the remaining 1/2 cup of flour until the dough pulls away from the sides of the bowl.
3. **Knead and Rise:**
    - Knead the dough for 5-7 minutes on a lightly floured surface or with the dough hook on medium speed, until smooth and elastic.
    - Place the dough in a greased bowl, cover with a clean kitchen towel, and let it rise in a warm place for about 1 to 1.5 hours, or until doubled in size.
4. **Prepare Filling:**
    - In a small bowl, combine brown sugar and cinnamon for the filling.

- Punch down the risen dough and roll it out on a lightly floured surface into a 16x21 inch rectangle.
- Spread the softened butter evenly over the dough, then sprinkle the cinnamon-sugar mixture over the butter.

5. **Roll and Cut:**
    - Starting with the long edge, tightly roll up the dough into a log. Pinch the seam to seal.
    - Cut the rolled dough into 12 equal pieces using a sharp knife or dental floss.
6. **Arrange and Rise:**
    - Place the rolls in a greased 9x13 inch baking dish or two 9-inch round cake pans.
    - Cover the rolls with a clean kitchen towel and let them rise again in a warm place for 30-45 minutes, or until doubled in size.
7. **Bake:**
    - Preheat the oven to 375°F (190°C).
    - Bake the cinnamon rolls for 25-30 minutes, or until golden brown.
8. **Make Frosting:**
    - While the rolls are baking, prepare the cream cheese frosting. In a medium bowl, beat together the softened cream cheese and butter until smooth.
    - Add powdered sugar, vanilla extract, and a pinch of salt. Beat until creamy and smooth.
9. **Frost and Serve:**
    - Allow the cinnamon rolls to cool for a few minutes in the pan, then spread the cream cheese frosting over them while they are still warm.
    - Serve the cinnamon rolls warm and enjoy!

These homemade cinnamon rolls are wonderfully soft, gooey, and aromatic—a perfect treat for any breakfast or brunch occasion!

Banana Pancakes

Ingredients:

- 1 cup all-purpose flour
- 1 tablespoon granulated sugar
- 2 teaspoons baking powder
- 1/4 teaspoon salt
- 1 ripe banana, mashed
- 1 large egg
- 1 cup milk
- 2 tablespoons unsalted butter, melted
- 1 teaspoon vanilla extract
- Optional: Sliced bananas, chopped nuts, chocolate chips for topping

Instructions:

1. **Mix Dry Ingredients:**
   - In a large bowl, whisk together the flour, sugar, baking powder, and salt.
2. **Prepare Wet Ingredients:**
   - In another bowl, mash the ripe banana with a fork until smooth. Add the egg, milk, melted butter, and vanilla extract. Whisk until well combined.
3. **Combine Wet and Dry Ingredients:**
   - Pour the wet ingredients into the bowl of dry ingredients. Stir gently until just combined. It's okay if the batter is slightly lumpy. Do not overmix.
4. **Cook Pancakes:**
   - Heat a non-stick skillet or griddle over medium heat. Lightly grease with butter or oil.
   - Pour 1/4 cup of batter onto the skillet for each pancake. Use the back of a spoon to spread the batter into a round shape if needed.
   - Cook the pancakes for 2-3 minutes, or until bubbles form on the surface and the edges look set.
5. **Flip and Cook:**
   - Carefully flip the pancakes with a spatula and cook for an additional 1-2 minutes, or until golden brown and cooked through.
6. **Serve:**
   - Stack the banana pancakes on a plate. Top with sliced bananas, chopped nuts, chocolate chips, or your favorite toppings.
   - Drizzle with maple syrup or honey, if desired.

Enjoy your homemade banana pancakes as a delightful breakfast treat! The natural sweetness from the bananas adds a wonderful flavor and moisture to the pancakes.

Huevos Rancheros

Ingredients:

- 4 large eggs
- 4 corn tortillas
- 1 cup refried beans (canned or homemade)
- 1 cup salsa (store-bought or homemade)
- 1/2 cup shredded cheese (cheddar, Monterey Jack, or Mexican blend)
- 1/4 cup chopped fresh cilantro (optional, for garnish)
- Salt and pepper, to taste
- Optional toppings: diced avocado, sliced jalapeños, sour cream, lime wedges

Instructions:

1. **Prepare Tortillas:**
   - Heat a non-stick skillet over medium heat. Warm each corn tortilla for about 30 seconds on each side until pliable and slightly toasted. Set aside and keep warm.
2. **Cook Eggs:**
   - In the same skillet, cook the eggs sunny-side up or however you prefer. Season with salt and pepper.
3. **Heat Refried Beans:**
   - Heat the refried beans in a small saucepan or in the microwave until warm.
4. **Assemble Huevos Rancheros:**
   - Spread a generous spoonful of warmed refried beans onto each corn tortilla, spreading it evenly.
   - Place a cooked egg on top of the beans on each tortilla.
5. **Add Salsa and Cheese:**
   - Spoon salsa over each egg, covering the egg and tortilla evenly.
   - Sprinkle shredded cheese over the salsa.
6. **Garnish and Serve:**
   - Garnish with chopped cilantro, if desired, and any additional toppings such as diced avocado, sliced jalapeños, sour cream, or a squeeze of fresh lime juice.
   - Serve immediately while warm and enjoy your flavorful Huevos Rancheros!

This dish is hearty and flavorful, perfect for a satisfying breakfast or brunch. Adjust the toppings and spice level to your liking for a personalized Huevos Rancheros experience.

Sausage Gravy and Biscuits

Ingredients:

For the biscuits:

- 2 cups all-purpose flour
- 1 tablespoon baking powder
- 1 teaspoon salt
- 1/2 cup unsalted butter, cold and cut into cubes
- 3/4 cup milk

For the sausage gravy:

- 1/2 lb breakfast sausage (pork or turkey)
- 1/4 cup all-purpose flour
- 2 cups milk
- Salt and pepper, to taste
- Optional: Dash of cayenne pepper or paprika for a bit of heat

Instructions:

1. **Make the Biscuits:**
   - Preheat your oven to 425°F (220°C).
   - In a large bowl, whisk together the flour, baking powder, and salt.
   - Cut in the cold butter using a pastry cutter or fork until the mixture resembles coarse crumbs.
   - Gradually add the milk, stirring until the dough comes together. It should be soft and slightly sticky.
   - Turn the dough out onto a lightly floured surface and knead gently a few times. Roll or pat the dough to about 1/2 inch thick.
   - Use a round cutter or a drinking glass to cut out biscuits. Place them on a baking sheet lined with parchment paper.
   - Bake for 12-15 minutes, or until the biscuits are golden brown on top.
2. **Make the Sausage Gravy:**
   - While the biscuits are baking, cook the sausage in a large skillet over medium heat. Break it up with a spatula as it cooks until browned and cooked through.
   - Sprinkle flour over the cooked sausage and stir well to coat. Cook for 1-2 minutes, stirring constantly.
   - Gradually pour in the milk, stirring constantly to prevent lumps from forming. Continue cooking and stirring until the gravy thickens and comes to a simmer.
   - Reduce heat to low and let the gravy simmer for a few minutes until it reaches your desired thickness. Season with salt, pepper, and a dash of cayenne pepper or paprika for additional flavor if desired.
3. **Assemble and Serve:**

- Split the warm biscuits in half and place them on serving plates.
  - Ladle the hot sausage gravy over the biscuits.
  - Serve immediately and enjoy this comforting breakfast dish!

Sausage gravy and biscuits are a hearty and delicious breakfast option that's perfect for weekends or special occasions. The creamy gravy paired with fluffy biscuits is sure to be a hit at the breakfast table!

Quiche Lorraine

Ingredients:

For the crust:

- 1 and 1/4 cups all-purpose flour
- 1/2 teaspoon salt
- 1/2 cup unsalted butter, cold and cut into cubes
- 3-4 tablespoons ice water

For the filling:

- 6 slices bacon, chopped
- 1 cup shredded Swiss cheese (Gruyère or Emmental)
- 1/2 cup chopped onion
- 4 large eggs
- 1 cup heavy cream
- 1/2 cup milk (whole or 2%)
- Salt and pepper, to taste
- Pinch of nutmeg (optional)

Instructions:

1. **Make the Crust:**
    - In a food processor, pulse together the flour and salt.
    - Add the cold butter cubes and pulse until the mixture resembles coarse crumbs.
    - Gradually add the ice water, 1 tablespoon at a time, pulsing until the dough just comes together.
    - Shape the dough into a disc, wrap it in plastic wrap, and refrigerate for at least 1 hour.
2. **Preheat the Oven:**
    - Preheat your oven to 375°F (190°C).
3. **Prepare the Filling:**
    - In a skillet, cook the chopped bacon over medium heat until crisp. Remove with a slotted spoon and drain on paper towels.
    - In the same skillet, sauté the chopped onion until softened and translucent. Remove from heat.
4. **Roll Out and Line the Crust:**
    - On a lightly floured surface, roll out the chilled dough into a circle about 12 inches in diameter.
    - Carefully transfer the dough to a 9-inch pie dish. Press it gently into the bottom and sides of the dish. Trim any excess dough and crimp the edges.
5. **Assemble and Bake:**

- Sprinkle the cooked bacon, sautéed onion, and shredded Swiss cheese evenly over the bottom of the pie crust.
- In a bowl, whisk together the eggs, heavy cream, milk, salt, pepper, and nutmeg (if using) until well combined.
- Pour the egg mixture over the bacon, onion, and cheese in the pie crust.

6. **Bake the Quiche:**
    - Place the quiche on a baking sheet (to catch any drips) and bake in the preheated oven for 35-40 minutes, or until the quiche is set and the top is golden brown.
    - Remove from the oven and let it cool slightly before slicing and serving.

7. **Serve:**
    - Quiche Lorraine can be served warm or at room temperature. It makes a delightful brunch dish or light dinner when paired with a green salad.

Enjoy your homemade Quiche Lorraine with its creamy, cheesy, and bacon-filled goodness!

Breakfast Potatoes

Ingredients:

- 4 medium potatoes (such as Russet or Yukon Gold), washed and diced into small cubes
- 2 tablespoons olive oil or melted butter
- 1 teaspoon paprika
- 1/2 teaspoon garlic powder
- 1/2 teaspoon onion powder
- 1/2 teaspoon dried thyme (optional)
- Salt and pepper, to taste
- Fresh parsley or chives, chopped (optional, for garnish)

Instructions:

1. **Preheat Oven:**
   - Preheat your oven to 400°F (200°C). Line a large baking sheet with parchment paper or aluminum foil for easy cleanup.
2. **Prepare Potatoes:**
   - Wash the potatoes well and pat them dry with a clean kitchen towel. Cut them into small cubes, about 1/2 inch to 3/4 inch in size.
3. **Season Potatoes:**
   - In a large bowl, toss the diced potatoes with olive oil or melted butter until evenly coated.
   - Add paprika, garlic powder, onion powder, dried thyme (if using), salt, and pepper. Toss again until the potatoes are well coated with the seasoning.
4. **Bake Potatoes:**
   - Spread the seasoned potatoes in a single layer on the prepared baking sheet.
   - Bake in the preheated oven for 30-35 minutes, stirring halfway through, until the potatoes are golden brown and crispy on the outside, and fork-tender on the inside.
5. **Serve:**
   - Transfer the baked breakfast potatoes to a serving dish. Sprinkle with chopped fresh parsley or chives for garnish, if desired.
   - Serve hot alongside scrambled eggs, bacon, sausage, or your favorite breakfast dishes.

These crispy and seasoned breakfast potatoes are perfect for starting your day with a delicious and satisfying breakfast. Adjust the seasonings to your taste and enjoy!

Corned Beef Hash

Ingredients:

- 2 cups cooked corned beef, diced (leftover from a boiled dinner or canned)
- 2 cups potatoes, diced (about 2 medium potatoes)
- 1 small onion, diced
- 1 tablespoon vegetable oil or butter
- Salt and pepper, to taste
- Optional: 1/2 bell pepper, diced
- Optional: Chopped fresh parsley or green onions for garnish

Instructions:

1. **Prepare Potatoes:**
    - If using raw potatoes, peel and dice them into small cubes. Place the diced potatoes in a medium saucepan, cover with water, and bring to a boil. Cook for about 5 minutes, until just tender. Drain and set aside.
2. **Cook Onions:**
    - In a large skillet, heat the vegetable oil or melt the butter over medium heat. Add the diced onion (and bell pepper, if using) and sauté until softened and translucent, about 5 minutes.
3. **Combine Ingredients:**
    - Add the diced corned beef and cooked potatoes to the skillet with the onions. Season with salt and pepper to taste.
4. **Cook Hash:**
    - Spread the mixture evenly in the skillet and press down gently with a spatula. Cook undisturbed for 5-7 minutes, or until the bottom is crispy and browned.
    - Use a spatula to flip sections of the hash to crisp the other side. Cook for an additional 5-7 minutes, or until the potatoes are golden brown and crispy.
5. **Serve:**
    - Transfer the corned beef hash to serving plates or a serving dish. Garnish with chopped fresh parsley or green onions if desired.
    - Serve hot, optionally with fried or poached eggs on top for a complete breakfast.

Corned beef hash is a delicious way to use leftover corned beef and potatoes, creating a flavorful and satisfying breakfast or brunch dish. Adjust the seasonings and add your favorite vegetables to personalize this comforting meal.

Belgian Waffles

Ingredients:

- 2 cups all-purpose flour
- 1/4 cup granulated sugar
- 1 tablespoon baking powder
- 1/2 teaspoon salt
- 1 and 3/4 cups milk
- 2 large eggs
- 1/2 cup unsalted butter, melted
- 1 teaspoon vanilla extract

Instructions:

1. **Preheat Waffle Iron:**
    - Preheat your Belgian waffle iron according to manufacturer's instructions.
2. **Prepare Batter:**
    - In a large bowl, whisk together the flour, sugar, baking powder, and salt.
3. **Mix Wet Ingredients:**
    - In another bowl, whisk together the milk, eggs, melted butter, and vanilla extract until well combined.
4. **Combine Wet and Dry Ingredients:**
    - Pour the wet ingredients into the bowl of dry ingredients. Stir until just combined; the batter may be slightly lumpy, but avoid overmixing.
5. **Cook Waffles:**
    - Lightly grease the preheated waffle iron with non-stick cooking spray or brush with melted butter.
    - Pour enough batter onto the hot waffle iron to cover the grids (amount will depend on your waffle iron size).
    - Close the lid and cook according to the manufacturer's instructions, typically 3-5 minutes, or until the waffles are golden brown and crisp.
6. **Serve:**
    - Carefully remove the waffles from the iron and serve immediately while warm.
    - Serve Belgian waffles with your favorite toppings such as fresh berries, whipped cream, maple syrup, powdered sugar, or chocolate sauce.
7. **Variations:**
    - For chocolate Belgian waffles, add 1/2 cup cocoa powder to the dry ingredients and increase the sugar to 1/2 cup.
    - For savory waffles, omit the sugar and vanilla extract and add herbs, cheese, or cooked bacon to the batter.

Enjoy your homemade Belgian waffles for a delightful breakfast or brunch treat! Adjust toppings and additions according to your taste preferences for a personalized waffle experience.

Biscuits and Gravy

Ingredients:

For the biscuits:

- 2 cups all-purpose flour
- 1 tablespoon baking powder
- 1/2 teaspoon baking soda
- 1 teaspoon salt
- 1/2 cup unsalted butter, cold and cut into cubes
- 3/4 cup buttermilk (or milk with 1 tablespoon of vinegar or lemon juice)

For the sausage gravy:

- 1/2 lb breakfast sausage (pork or turkey)
- 1/4 cup all-purpose flour
- 2 cups milk
- Salt and pepper, to taste
- Optional: Dash of cayenne pepper for a bit of heat

Instructions:

1. **Make the Biscuits:**
    - Preheat your oven to 450°F (230°C). Line a baking sheet with parchment paper.
    - In a large bowl, whisk together the flour, baking powder, baking soda, and salt.
    - Cut in the cold butter using a pastry cutter or fork until the mixture resembles coarse crumbs.
    - Gradually add the buttermilk, stirring until the dough comes together. It should be soft and slightly sticky.
    - Turn the dough out onto a lightly floured surface and knead gently a few times. Pat or roll the dough to about 1-inch thickness.
    - Use a round cutter or a drinking glass to cut out biscuits. Place them on the prepared baking sheet, leaving a little space between each biscuit.
    - Bake for 10-12 minutes, or until the biscuits are golden brown on top.
2. **Make the Sausage Gravy:**
    - While the biscuits are baking, cook the sausage in a large skillet over medium heat. Break it up with a spatula as it cooks until browned and cooked through.
    - Sprinkle flour over the cooked sausage and stir well to coat. Cook for 1-2 minutes, stirring constantly.
    - Gradually pour in the milk, stirring constantly to prevent lumps from forming. Continue cooking and stirring until the gravy thickens and comes to a simmer.
    - Reduce heat to low and let the gravy simmer for a few minutes until it reaches your desired thickness. Season with salt, pepper, and cayenne pepper (if using).
3. **Serve:**

- Split the warm biscuits in half and place them on serving plates.
- Spoon generous amounts of sausage gravy over each biscuit.
- Serve immediately while warm.

Enjoy your homemade biscuits and gravy as a comforting and satisfying breakfast or brunch dish!

Breakfast Tacos

Ingredients:

- 8 small corn or flour tortillas
- 6 large eggs
- 1 tablespoon butter or oil
- Salt and pepper, to taste
- 1 cup cooked breakfast sausage, chopped (or bacon, ham, chorizo, etc.)
- 1 cup shredded cheese (cheddar, Monterey Jack, or Mexican blend)
- Optional toppings: Salsa, diced tomatoes, avocado slices, sour cream, chopped cilantro, hot sauce

Instructions:

1. **Prepare Tortillas:**
   - Warm the tortillas in a dry skillet over medium heat for about 30 seconds on each side, or wrap them in foil and heat in a low oven until warm.
2. **Cook Eggs:**
   - In a large skillet, melt butter or heat oil over medium heat.
   - Crack the eggs into a bowl, season with salt and pepper, and whisk until well combined.
   - Pour the eggs into the skillet and cook, stirring occasionally with a spatula, until scrambled and just set. Remove from heat.
3. **Assemble Tacos:**
   - Spoon scrambled eggs onto each warm tortilla.
   - Top with cooked breakfast sausage (or your choice of protein).
   - Sprinkle shredded cheese over the eggs and sausage.
4. **Add Toppings:**
   - Garnish with your favorite toppings such as salsa, diced tomatoes, avocado slices, sour cream, chopped cilantro, or hot sauce.
5. **Serve:**
   - Serve the breakfast tacos immediately while warm.
   - Optionally, serve with additional sides like refried beans or breakfast potatoes.

Enjoy these delicious and customizable breakfast tacos for a hearty start to your day! They're perfect for brunch gatherings or a quick and satisfying breakfast on the go.

Oatmeal with Fruit

Ingredients:

- 1 cup rolled oats (old-fashioned oats)
- 2 cups water or milk (dairy milk, almond milk, soy milk, etc.)
- Pinch of salt
- 1/2 teaspoon ground cinnamon (optional)
- 1 ripe banana, mashed (optional for added sweetness and creaminess)
- Fresh fruits: Choose from berries (strawberries, blueberries, raspberries), sliced bananas, sliced apples, diced peaches, or any fruit of your choice
- Optional toppings: Honey, maple syrup, chopped nuts (almonds, walnuts, pecans), chia seeds, flaxseeds, coconut flakes

Instructions:

1. **Cook Oatmeal:**
    - In a medium saucepan, bring the water or milk to a boil over medium-high heat.
    - Stir in the rolled oats and reduce the heat to medium-low.
    - Add a pinch of salt and ground cinnamon (if using). Stir occasionally and cook for about 5 minutes, or until the oats are tender and the mixture has thickened to your desired consistency.
2. **Add Mashed Banana (Optional):**
    - If using mashed banana, stir it into the oatmeal during the last minute of cooking to incorporate it well.
3. **Prepare Fruit:**
    - While the oatmeal is cooking, prepare your choice of fresh fruits. Wash and slice or dice them as needed.
4. **Serve:**
    - Once the oatmeal is cooked to your liking, remove from heat.
    - Divide the oatmeal into serving bowls.
    - Top each bowl with a generous amount of fresh fruits.
5. **Add Toppings:**
    - Drizzle honey or maple syrup over the oatmeal and fruits, if desired.
    - Sprinkle chopped nuts, chia seeds, flaxseeds, or coconut flakes on top for added texture and nutrition.
6. **Enjoy:**
    - Serve the oatmeal with fruit immediately while warm.
    - Stir everything together before eating to combine the flavors of the oatmeal and fresh fruits.

This oatmeal with fruit recipe is versatile and can be adjusted based on your taste preferences and the fruits available to you. It's a delicious and nutritious breakfast option that provides energy and essential nutrients to start your day right.

Bagels with Lox

Ingredients:

- 4 bagels (plain, sesame, or your favorite variety)
- 8 oz smoked salmon (lox), thinly sliced
- 1/2 cup cream cheese, softened
- 1 tablespoon capers, drained
- 1/2 red onion, thinly sliced
- Fresh dill, for garnish
- Lemon wedges, for serving
- Optional: Sliced tomatoes, cucumber, avocado, or lettuce

Instructions:

1. **Prepare Bagels:**
   - Slice the bagels in half horizontally using a serrated knife.
2. **Toast Bagels (Optional):**
   - Toast the bagel halves lightly in a toaster or toaster oven, if desired.
3. **Spread Cream Cheese:**
   - Spread a generous amount of softened cream cheese on each toasted bagel half.
4. **Assemble Bagels:**
   - Arrange slices of smoked salmon (lox) on top of the cream cheese on each bagel half.
5. **Add Toppings:**
   - Sprinkle capers over the smoked salmon.
   - Place a few slices of red onion on top.
6. **Garnish:**
   - Garnish with fresh dill sprigs for added flavor and presentation.
7. **Serve:**
   - Serve the bagels with lox immediately, accompanied by lemon wedges on the side.
   - Optionally, serve with additional toppings such as sliced tomatoes, cucumber, avocado, or lettuce.

Bagels with lox are traditionally served open-faced, allowing you to fully appreciate the flavors of the smoked salmon, creamy cream cheese, and tangy capers. It's a delicious and satisfying breakfast or brunch option that's sure to be enjoyed by everyone!

Scrambled Eggs with Smoked Salmon

Ingredients:

- 4 large eggs
- 2 tablespoons milk or cream
- Salt and pepper, to taste
- 2 tablespoons unsalted butter
- 2 oz smoked salmon, chopped into small pieces
- Chopped fresh dill, for garnish
- Optional: Toasted bread or bagels for serving

Instructions:

1. **Prepare Eggs:**
    - In a bowl, whisk together the eggs, milk or cream, salt, and pepper until well combined.
2. **Cook Eggs:**
    - In a non-stick skillet, melt the butter over medium-low heat.
    - Pour the egg mixture into the skillet and let it sit undisturbed for a few seconds until the edges start to set.
3. **Scramble Eggs:**
    - Using a spatula, gently stir and fold the eggs from the edges towards the center of the skillet. Continue cooking and stirring occasionally until the eggs are mostly set but still slightly runny.
4. **Add Smoked Salmon:**
    - Add the chopped smoked salmon to the skillet with the scrambled eggs. Continue cooking for another minute or so, stirring gently, until the eggs are fully cooked and the salmon is heated through.
5. **Garnish and Serve:**
    - Remove the skillet from heat.
    - Sprinkle chopped fresh dill over the scrambled eggs and smoked salmon for added flavor and freshness.
6. **Serve:**
    - Serve the scrambled eggs with smoked salmon immediately, optionally with toasted bread or bagels on the side.

Enjoy your creamy and savory scrambled eggs with the delightful addition of smoked salmon. It's a delicious breakfast or brunch option that's quick to prepare and sure to impress!

Cinnamon French Toast

Ingredients:

- 4 slices of bread (such as white, whole wheat, brioche, or challah)
- 2 large eggs
- 1/2 cup milk (whole milk or any milk of your choice)
- 1 teaspoon ground cinnamon
- 1/2 teaspoon vanilla extract
- 1 tablespoon granulated sugar (optional, for added sweetness)
- Butter or oil, for cooking
- Optional toppings: Maple syrup, powdered sugar, fresh berries, sliced bananas, whipped cream

Instructions:

1. **Prepare Bread:**
   - In a shallow bowl or pie plate, whisk together the eggs, milk, ground cinnamon, vanilla extract, and sugar (if using) until well combined.
2. **Soak Bread:**
   - Dip each slice of bread into the egg mixture, turning to coat both sides evenly. Allow the bread to soak for about 10-15 seconds per side, ensuring it absorbs the mixture without becoming too soggy.
3. **Cook French Toast:**
   - In a large non-stick skillet or griddle, melt a small amount of butter or heat a little oil over medium heat.
   - Place the soaked bread slices onto the skillet or griddle. Cook for 2-3 minutes on each side, or until golden brown and cooked through.
4. **Serve:**
   - Transfer the cooked cinnamon French toast to serving plates.
   - Serve warm with your favorite toppings such as maple syrup, powdered sugar, fresh berries, sliced bananas, or whipped cream.
5. **Enjoy:**
   - Enjoy your homemade cinnamon French toast as a delicious and satisfying breakfast or brunch treat!

This recipe is versatile, allowing you to adjust the sweetness and spice level to your preference. It's perfect for a leisurely weekend breakfast or as a special treat for family and friends.

Avocado Toast with Poached Eggs

Ingredients:

- 2 slices of bread (sourdough, whole wheat, multigrain, or your favorite variety)
- 1 ripe avocado
- Juice of half a lemon
- Salt and pepper, to taste
- 2 large eggs
- Optional toppings: Red pepper flakes, paprika, cherry tomatoes, arugula, microgreens, crumbled feta cheese

Instructions:

1. **Prepare Avocado Spread:**
    - Cut the avocado in half and remove the pit. Scoop the flesh into a bowl.
    - Add lemon juice, salt, and pepper to taste. Mash the avocado with a fork until creamy but still slightly chunky.
2. **Toast Bread:**
    - Toast the bread slices until golden brown and crispy.
3. **Poach Eggs:**
    - Fill a medium-sized saucepan with water and bring it to a gentle simmer over medium heat.
    - Crack each egg into a small bowl or cup.
    - Create a gentle whirlpool in the simmering water using a spoon. Carefully slide each egg into the center of the whirlpool.
    - Poach the eggs for about 3-4 minutes, until the whites are set but the yolks are still runny.
    - Remove the poached eggs with a slotted spoon and drain on a paper towel.
4. **Assemble Avocado Toast:**
    - Spread the mashed avocado evenly onto each slice of toasted bread.
    - Place a poached egg on top of each slice of avocado toast.
5. **Add Toppings:**
    - Sprinkle with red pepper flakes, paprika, or any other desired toppings.
    - Optionally, add cherry tomatoes, arugula, microgreens, or crumbled feta cheese for extra flavor and texture.
6. **Serve:**
    - Serve avocado toast with poached eggs immediately while warm.
    - Enjoy this delicious and nutritious breakfast or brunch dish!

Avocado toast with poached eggs is not only delicious but also packed with healthy fats, proteins, and nutrients. It's a versatile dish that can be customized to your liking with different toppings and seasonings.

Breakfast Quesadillas

Ingredients:

- 4 large flour tortillas
- 1 cup shredded cheese (cheddar, Monterey Jack, or a Mexican cheese blend)
- 4 large eggs
- 1/2 cup diced cooked bacon or sausage (optional)
- 1/2 cup diced bell peppers (any color)
- 1/4 cup diced red onion
- Salt and pepper, to taste
- 2 tablespoons butter or oil, divided
- Optional toppings: Salsa, sour cream, guacamole, chopped cilantro

Instructions:

1. **Prepare Ingredients:**
    - In a bowl, whisk the eggs together with salt and pepper. Set aside.
    - Heat a large skillet over medium heat and cook the bacon or sausage (if using) until browned and cooked through. Remove from skillet and drain excess fat if needed.
    - In the same skillet, add 1 tablespoon of butter or oil over medium heat. Sauté the diced bell peppers and red onion until softened, about 3-4 minutes. Remove from skillet and set aside.
2. **Cook Eggs:**
    - In the same skillet, add the remaining 1 tablespoon of butter or oil over medium heat.
    - Pour in the whisked eggs and cook, stirring occasionally with a spatula, until scrambled and just set. Remove from heat.
3. **Assemble Quesadillas:**
    - Heat a clean large skillet or griddle over medium heat.
    - Place one tortilla on the skillet and sprinkle with a quarter of the shredded cheese.
    - Layer with scrambled eggs, cooked bacon or sausage (if using), sautéed bell peppers and onions, and an additional sprinkle of cheese.
    - Top with another tortilla and press down gently with a spatula.
4. **Cook Quesadillas:**
    - Cook the quesadilla for about 2-3 minutes on each side, or until the tortilla is golden brown and the cheese is melted.
    - Repeat with the remaining tortillas and filling ingredients.
5. **Serve:**
    - Remove the cooked quesadillas from the skillet and let them cool slightly on a cutting board.
    - Cut each quesadilla into wedges using a pizza cutter or sharp knife.

- - Serve warm with optional toppings such as salsa, sour cream, guacamole, or chopped cilantro.

Enjoy your homemade breakfast quesadillas as a delicious and hearty breakfast or brunch option. They are versatile, so feel free to customize with your favorite breakfast ingredients and toppings!

Breakfast Pizza

Ingredients:

- 1 pound pizza dough (homemade or store-bought)
- 1/2 cup pizza sauce or marinara sauce
- 1 cup shredded mozzarella cheese
- 4 slices bacon, cooked and crumbled
- 4 large eggs
- Salt and pepper, to taste
- Optional toppings: Sliced bell peppers, sliced mushrooms, chopped onions, cherry tomatoes, spinach, cooked breakfast sausage

Instructions:

1. **Preheat Oven:**
   - Preheat your oven to 475°F (245°C). If using a pizza stone, place it in the oven to preheat as well.
2. **Prepare Pizza Dough:**
   - On a lightly floured surface, roll out the pizza dough into a circle or rectangle, about 1/4 inch thick. Transfer the dough to a parchment-lined baking sheet or pizza peel dusted with cornmeal.
3. **Assemble Pizza:**
   - Spread the pizza sauce evenly over the dough, leaving a small border around the edges.
   - Sprinkle shredded mozzarella cheese over the sauce.
   - Distribute cooked bacon evenly over the cheese.
4. **Prepare Eggs:**
   - Create four wells or indentations on the pizza using the back of a spoon or your fingers.
   - Crack an egg into each well, being careful not to break the yolks. Season with salt and pepper.
5. **Bake Pizza:**
   - Carefully transfer the pizza to the preheated oven (onto the pizza stone, if using).
   - Bake for 10-12 minutes, or until the crust is golden brown, the cheese is melted and bubbly, and the egg whites are set but the yolks are still slightly runny.
6. **Finish and Serve:**
   - Remove the breakfast pizza from the oven and let it cool for a few minutes.
   - Optional: Sprinkle additional toppings such as sliced bell peppers, cherry tomatoes, or chopped fresh herbs over the pizza.
   - Slice the pizza into wedges and serve hot.

Enjoy your homemade breakfast pizza as a delicious and hearty meal to start your day! Feel free to customize the toppings according to your taste preferences and favorite breakfast ingredients.

Hash Brown Casserole

Ingredients:

- 1 package (30 oz) frozen shredded hash brown potatoes, thawed
- 1 can (10.5 oz) condensed cream of chicken soup (or cream of mushroom soup)
- 1 and 1/2 cups sour cream
- 1/2 cup unsalted butter, melted
- 1 small onion, finely chopped
- 2 cups shredded cheddar cheese (or your favorite cheese blend)
- 1 teaspoon salt
- 1/2 teaspoon black pepper
- Optional topping: 1 cup crushed cornflakes mixed with 2 tablespoons melted butter (for a crunchy topping)

Instructions:

1. **Preheat Oven:**
    - Preheat your oven to 350°F (175°C). Grease a 9x13 inch baking dish with butter or non-stick cooking spray.
2. **Mix Ingredients:**
    - In a large bowl, combine the thawed hash brown potatoes, cream of chicken soup, sour cream, melted butter, chopped onion, shredded cheese, salt, and black pepper. Mix until well combined.
3. **Assemble Casserole:**
    - Spread the potato mixture evenly into the prepared baking dish.
4. **Optional Crunchy Topping:**
    - If using the optional topping, mix the crushed cornflakes with melted butter in a small bowl. Sprinkle evenly over the top of the casserole.
5. **Bake:**
    - Cover the casserole dish with aluminum foil and bake in the preheated oven for 45 minutes.
    - Remove the foil and continue baking for an additional 15-20 minutes, or until the casserole is bubbly and the top is golden brown.
6. **Serve:**
    - Remove from the oven and let the hash brown casserole cool for a few minutes before serving.
    - Serve warm as a delicious side dish or as part of a breakfast or brunch spread.

This hash brown casserole recipe is versatile and can be customized by adding diced ham, cooked bacon, or chopped vegetables like bell peppers or spinach. It's a crowd-pleasing dish that's perfect for feeding a family or for potlucks and gatherings. Enjoy the creamy, cheesy goodness of this comforting casserole!

Veggie Frittata

Ingredients:

- 8 large eggs
- 1/4 cup milk or heavy cream
- Salt and pepper, to taste
- 1 tablespoon olive oil
- 1 small onion, diced
- 1 bell pepper, diced (any color)
- 1 cup sliced mushrooms
- 1 cup spinach leaves, chopped
- 1/2 cup cherry tomatoes, halved
- 1/2 cup shredded cheese (cheddar, mozzarella, feta, or your choice)
- Optional: Fresh herbs (such as parsley, basil, or thyme) for garnish

Instructions:

1. **Preheat Oven:**
   - Preheat your oven to 350°F (175°C).
2. **Prepare Vegetables:**
   - In a large oven-safe skillet, heat olive oil over medium heat. Add diced onion and bell pepper, and sauté for 3-4 minutes until softened.
   - Add sliced mushrooms to the skillet and cook for another 2-3 minutes until they begin to soften.
3. **Add Spinach and Tomatoes:**
   - Add chopped spinach leaves and halved cherry tomatoes to the skillet. Cook for 1-2 minutes until the spinach wilts slightly. Season with salt and pepper to taste. Remove from heat.
4. **Whisk Eggs:**
   - In a large bowl, whisk together eggs, milk or cream, salt, and pepper until well combined.
5. **Assemble Frittata:**
   - Pour the whisked egg mixture evenly over the sautéed vegetables in the skillet. Gently stir to distribute the vegetables evenly in the egg mixture.
   - Sprinkle shredded cheese evenly over the top of the frittata.
6. **Bake:**
   - Transfer the skillet to the preheated oven. Bake for 20-25 minutes, or until the frittata is set in the center and the edges are lightly golden brown.
7. **Serve:**
   - Remove the frittata from the oven and let it cool for a few minutes.
   - Garnish with fresh herbs if desired. Slice into wedges and serve warm.

Enjoy your veggie frittata as a delicious and nutritious meal! It can be served on its own or with a side salad, crusty bread, or even roasted potatoes for a complete meal. This recipe is easily customizable with your favorite vegetables and cheeses, making it a versatile dish for any occasion.

Pumpkin Pancakes

Ingredients:

- 1 cup all-purpose flour
- 1 tablespoon granulated sugar
- 1 teaspoon baking powder
- 1/2 teaspoon baking soda
- 1/2 teaspoon salt
- 1 teaspoon pumpkin pie spice (or a mix of cinnamon, nutmeg, ginger, and cloves)
- 3/4 cup buttermilk (or milk)
- 1/2 cup pumpkin puree
- 1 large egg
- 2 tablespoons melted butter (plus more for cooking)
- Optional: Maple syrup, whipped cream, chopped nuts, or powdered sugar for serving

Instructions:

1. **Mix Dry Ingredients:**
   - In a large bowl, whisk together flour, sugar, baking powder, baking soda, salt, and pumpkin pie spice until well combined.
2. **Combine Wet Ingredients:**
   - In another bowl, whisk together buttermilk, pumpkin puree, egg, and melted butter until smooth.
3. **Combine Batter:**
   - Pour the wet ingredients into the dry ingredients. Stir gently until just combined. Do not overmix; a few lumps are okay. Let the batter rest for 5-10 minutes.
4. **Cook Pancakes:**
   - Heat a griddle or large non-stick skillet over medium heat. Lightly grease with butter or cooking spray.
   - Pour about 1/4 cup of batter for each pancake onto the griddle. Cook until bubbles form on the surface of the pancake and the edges look set, about 2-3 minutes.
   - Flip the pancakes and cook for another 1-2 minutes until golden brown and cooked through.
5. **Serve:**
   - Serve the pumpkin pancakes warm with your favorite toppings such as maple syrup, whipped cream, chopped nuts, or powdered sugar.

Enjoy these delicious pumpkin pancakes as a cozy and flavorful breakfast treat during the fall season or any time of the year! Adjust the spices or sweetness according to your taste preferences for a perfect breakfast delight.

Baked Oatmeal

Ingredients:

- 2 cups old-fashioned rolled oats
- 1/3 cup brown sugar (adjust to taste)
- 1 teaspoon baking powder
- 1 teaspoon ground cinnamon
- 1/2 teaspoon salt
- 2 cups milk (dairy milk, almond milk, soy milk, etc.)
- 1/4 cup melted butter or oil (such as coconut oil or vegetable oil)
- 2 large eggs
- 1 teaspoon vanilla extract
- Optional add-ins: Fresh or dried fruit (e.g., berries, chopped apples, raisins), nuts (e.g., chopped almonds, pecans), seeds (e.g., chia seeds, flaxseeds)

Instructions:

1. **Preheat Oven:**
   - Preheat your oven to 350°F (175°C). Grease a 9x9 inch baking dish with butter or cooking spray.
2. **Mix Dry Ingredients:**
   - In a large bowl, combine oats, brown sugar, baking powder, ground cinnamon, and salt. Stir until evenly mixed.
3. **Combine Wet Ingredients:**
   - In another bowl, whisk together milk, melted butter or oil, eggs, and vanilla extract until well combined.
4. **Combine Mixtures:**
   - Pour the wet ingredients into the bowl with the dry ingredients. Stir until everything is thoroughly combined.
5. **Add Optional Add-Ins:**
   - Gently fold in any optional add-ins like fresh or dried fruit, nuts, or seeds.
6. **Bake:**
   - Pour the mixture into the prepared baking dish, spreading it out evenly.
   - Bake in the preheated oven for 35-40 minutes, or until the top is golden brown and the oatmeal is set.
7. **Serve:**
   - Remove from the oven and let it cool slightly before serving.
   - Serve warm, optionally with a drizzle of milk or yogurt on top.

Variations:

- **Apple Cinnamon:** Add chopped apples and extra cinnamon.
- **Blueberry Almond:** Add fresh or frozen blueberries and chopped almonds.
- **Pumpkin Spice:** Substitute some milk with pumpkin puree and add pumpkin pie spice.

Baked oatmeal can be stored in the refrigerator for several days and reheated in the microwave or oven. It's a hearty and wholesome breakfast that's sure to become a favorite!

Breakfast Skillet

Ingredients:

- 4-6 large eggs
- 2 cups diced potatoes (such as russet or Yukon gold)
- 1 small onion, diced
- 1 bell pepper, diced (any color)
- 1 cup diced cooked sausage or bacon (optional)
- 1 cup shredded cheddar cheese (or your favorite cheese)
- 2 tablespoons olive oil or butter
- Salt and pepper, to taste
- Optional toppings: Chopped green onions, fresh herbs (parsley or cilantro), salsa, sour cream

Instructions:

1. **Cook Potatoes:**
   - Heat 1 tablespoon of olive oil or butter in a large skillet (cast iron works well) over medium heat.
   - Add diced potatoes to the skillet. Cook, stirring occasionally, until the potatoes are golden brown and cooked through, about 10-12 minutes. Season with salt and pepper to taste. Remove the potatoes from the skillet and set aside.
2. **Cook Vegetables:**
   - In the same skillet, add the remaining tablespoon of olive oil or butter.
   - Add diced onion and bell pepper to the skillet. Cook, stirring occasionally, until the vegetables are softened, about 5-7 minutes.
3. **Combine Ingredients:**
   - Return the cooked potatoes to the skillet with the cooked vegetables. Stir to combine.
4. **Add Protein (Optional):**
   - If using, add diced cooked sausage or bacon to the skillet. Stir to combine with the potatoes and vegetables.
5. **Prepare Eggs:**
   - Create 4-6 wells or indentations in the potato mixture using a spoon.
   - Crack an egg into each well. Season the eggs with salt and pepper.
6. **Cook Eggs:**
   - Cover the skillet with a lid or aluminum foil. Cook on medium-low heat for about 5-7 minutes, or until the eggs are cooked to your desired doneness (for runny yolks, cook for less time; for fully cooked yolks, cook longer).
7. **Add Cheese:**
   - Sprinkle shredded cheddar cheese evenly over the skillet. Cover again and let the cheese melt, about 1-2 minutes.
8. **Serve:**

- Remove the skillet from heat. Garnish with chopped green onions, fresh herbs, salsa, or sour cream if desired.
- Serve the breakfast skillet hot, directly from the skillet.

This breakfast skillet is versatile and can be customized with your favorite ingredients such as spinach, mushrooms, or different types of cheese. It's a hearty and satisfying breakfast that's perfect for feeding a family or a group of friends. Enjoy!

Lemon Poppy Seed Muffins

Ingredients:

- 2 cups all-purpose flour
- 3/4 cup granulated sugar
- 2 teaspoons baking powder
- 1/4 teaspoon baking soda
- 1/4 teaspoon salt
- Zest of 2 lemons
- 1/4 cup fresh lemon juice (from about 2 lemons)
- 1/2 cup unsalted butter, melted and cooled
- 3/4 cup buttermilk (or 3/4 cup milk + 1 tablespoon lemon juice or white vinegar, let sit for 5 minutes)
- 2 large eggs
- 1 teaspoon vanilla extract
- 2 tablespoons poppy seeds

Glaze (optional):

- 1/2 cup powdered sugar
- 1-2 tablespoons fresh lemon juice

Instructions:

1. **Preheat Oven and Prepare Muffin Pan:**
   - Preheat your oven to 375°F (190°C). Line a 12-cup muffin pan with paper liners or grease the cups with butter or cooking spray.
2. **Mix Dry Ingredients:**
   - In a large bowl, whisk together the flour, sugar, baking powder, baking soda, salt, and lemon zest.
3. **Combine Wet Ingredients:**
   - In another bowl, whisk together the melted butter, buttermilk, lemon juice, eggs, and vanilla extract until well combined.
4. **Combine Mixtures:**
   - Pour the wet ingredients into the bowl with the dry ingredients. Stir gently with a spatula until just combined. Do not overmix; it's okay if there are a few lumps.
   - Fold in the poppy seeds until evenly distributed throughout the batter.
5. **Fill Muffin Cups:**
   - Divide the batter evenly among the prepared muffin cups, filling each about 2/3 full.
6. **Bake:**
   - Bake in the preheated oven for 15-18 minutes, or until a toothpick inserted into the center of a muffin comes out clean or with a few crumbs attached.
7. **Cool Muffins:**

- Remove the muffin pan from the oven and place it on a wire rack. Let the muffins cool in the pan for 5 minutes, then transfer them to the wire rack to cool completely.
8. **Prepare Glaze (Optional):**
    - If desired, prepare the glaze by whisking together powdered sugar and lemon juice until smooth. Drizzle the glaze over the cooled muffins.
9. **Serve:**
    - Allow the glaze to set before serving the lemon poppy seed muffins.

Enjoy these lemon poppy seed muffins for breakfast, brunch, or as a delightful snack with a cup of tea or coffee. They are moist, flavorful, and perfect for any occasion!

Greek Yogurt Parfait

Ingredients:

- 1 cup Greek yogurt (plain or flavored, such as vanilla)
- 1/2 cup granola (homemade or store-bought)
- 1/2 cup mixed fresh berries (such as strawberries, blueberries, raspberries)
- 2 tablespoons chopped nuts (such as almonds, walnuts, or pecans)
- 1-2 tablespoons honey or maple syrup (optional, for sweetness)
- Optional add-ins: Chia seeds, flaxseeds, coconut flakes, dried fruit

Instructions:

1. **Prepare Yogurt:**
   - If using plain Greek yogurt, you can sweeten it by stirring in honey or maple syrup to taste. If using flavored Greek yogurt, skip this step.
2. **Layer Ingredients:**
   - Start by spooning a layer of Greek yogurt into the bottom of a glass or bowl.
   - Add a layer of granola on top of the yogurt. This adds crunch and texture.
3. **Add Fruit:**
   - Add a layer of mixed fresh berries or your choice of fruits on top of the granola layer. Make sure to distribute them evenly.
4. **Repeat Layers:**
   - Repeat the layers until you reach the top of the glass or bowl. You can add another layer of yogurt, followed by granola, and then top with more berries and nuts.
5. **Finish:**
   - Sprinkle chopped nuts and any additional toppings like chia seeds, flaxseeds, or coconut flakes on top.
6. **Serve:**
   - Drizzle with honey or maple syrup if desired for extra sweetness.
   - Serve the Greek yogurt parfait immediately as a nutritious breakfast or snack.

Variations:

- **Peanut Butter Banana:** Layer Greek yogurt with sliced bananas, peanut butter, and granola.
- **Tropical:** Use mango chunks, pineapple, and toasted coconut flakes.
- **Chocolate Lovers:** Add cocoa powder or chocolate chips to the Greek yogurt layers.

Greek yogurt parfaits are versatile and can be customized based on your preferences and the ingredients you have on hand. They are packed with protein, fiber, and healthy fats, making them a satisfying and nutritious choice for any time of day!

Breakfast Strata

Ingredients:

- 8 slices of bread (day-old bread works well), cubed
- 1 cup shredded cheddar cheese (or your favorite cheese)
- 1 cup diced cooked sausage or bacon (optional)
- 1 cup diced bell peppers (any color)
- 1 cup diced onion
- 1 cup diced mushrooms
- 1 cup spinach leaves, chopped
- 6 large eggs
- 2 cups milk (whole milk or any milk of your choice)
- 1 teaspoon Dijon mustard (optional)
- 1/2 teaspoon salt
- 1/4 teaspoon black pepper
- 1/4 teaspoon paprika (optional)
- Fresh herbs for garnish (such as parsley or chives)

Instructions:

1. **Prepare Ingredients:**
   - Grease a 9x13 inch baking dish with butter or cooking spray.
   - Cube the bread slices and spread them evenly in the prepared baking dish.
   - Sprinkle shredded cheese over the bread cubes. Add cooked sausage or bacon if using, and distribute evenly over the cheese.
2. **Prepare Vegetables:**
   - In a skillet, heat a little olive oil over medium heat.
   - Add diced bell peppers, onion, and mushrooms. Cook until softened, about 5-7 minutes.
   - Add chopped spinach and cook until wilted. Remove from heat and let cool slightly.
3. **Layer Vegetables:**
   - Spread the cooked vegetables evenly over the bread, cheese, and meat in the baking dish.
4. **Prepare Egg Mixture:**
   - In a large bowl, whisk together eggs, milk, Dijon mustard (if using), salt, pepper, and paprika until well combined.
5. **Pour Egg Mixture:**
   - Pour the egg mixture evenly over the layered ingredients in the baking dish. Press down lightly with a spoon to ensure the bread cubes absorb the egg mixture.
6. **Cover and Refrigerate:**
   - Cover the baking dish with aluminum foil or plastic wrap and refrigerate for at least 2 hours or overnight. This allows the bread to soak up the egg mixture.

7. **Bake:**
    - Preheat your oven to 350°F (175°C).
    - Remove the strata from the refrigerator and let it sit at room temperature while the oven heats up.
    - Bake, covered with foil, for 45 minutes. Then uncover and bake for an additional 15-20 minutes, or until the strata is set in the center and the top is golden brown.
8. **Serve:**
    - Remove from the oven and let it cool for a few minutes before serving.
    - Garnish with fresh herbs such as parsley or chives if desired.
    - Cut into squares and serve warm.

This breakfast strata can be served on its own or with a side of fresh fruit, salad, or roasted potatoes. It's a delicious and satisfying dish that's sure to impress your guests or family!

Apple Cinnamon Pancakes

Ingredients:

- 1 cup all-purpose flour
- 1 tablespoon granulated sugar
- 1 teaspoon baking powder
- 1/2 teaspoon baking soda
- 1/4 teaspoon salt
- 1 teaspoon ground cinnamon
- 3/4 cup buttermilk (or 3/4 cup milk + 1 tablespoon lemon juice or white vinegar, let sit for 5 minutes)
- 1/4 cup unsweetened applesauce
- 1 large egg
- 2 tablespoons unsalted butter, melted and cooled
- 1 teaspoon vanilla extract
- 1 medium apple, peeled, cored, and finely chopped (about 1 cup)
- Butter or oil for cooking pancakes

Optional toppings:

- Maple syrup
- Powdered sugar
- Additional chopped apples
- Chopped nuts (such as pecans or walnuts)

Instructions:

1. **Mix Dry Ingredients:**
   - In a large bowl, whisk together the flour, sugar, baking powder, baking soda, salt, and ground cinnamon.
2. **Combine Wet Ingredients:**
   - In another bowl, whisk together the buttermilk, applesauce, egg, melted butter, and vanilla extract until smooth.
3. **Combine Mixtures:**
   - Pour the wet ingredients into the bowl with the dry ingredients. Stir gently until just combined. Do not overmix; it's okay if there are a few lumps.
4. **Add Chopped Apples:**
   - Gently fold in the chopped apple pieces until evenly distributed throughout the batter.
5. **Cook Pancakes:**
   - Heat a griddle or large non-stick skillet over medium heat. Add a small amount of butter or oil to coat the surface.
   - Pour about 1/4 cup of batter for each pancake onto the griddle. Use the back of a spoon to spread the batter into a round shape if needed.

- - Cook for 2-3 minutes, or until bubbles form on the surface of the pancake and the edges look set.
  - Flip the pancakes and cook for another 1-2 minutes until golden brown and cooked through.
6. **Serve:**
    - Stack the pancakes on a plate and serve warm.
    - Optional: Serve with maple syrup, a dusting of powdered sugar, additional chopped apples, or chopped nuts on top.

Enjoy these fluffy and flavorful apple cinnamon pancakes for a cozy breakfast or brunch treat! They are perfect for celebrating fall flavors or any time you're craving a delicious pancake variation.

Monte Cristo Sandwich

Ingredients:

- 8 slices of bread (white or whole wheat)
- 8 slices of Swiss cheese
- 8 slices of deli ham (or turkey/chicken)
- Dijon mustard (optional)
- 3 large eggs
- 1/2 cup milk
- 1/4 teaspoon salt
- 1/4 teaspoon black pepper
- Butter or vegetable oil, for cooking
- Powdered sugar, for dusting (optional)
- Maple syrup or jam, for dipping (optional)

Instructions:

1. **Assemble the Sandwiches:**
   - Spread a thin layer of Dijon mustard on half of the bread slices (if using).
   - Layer each mustard-coated slice with a slice of Swiss cheese, then 2 slices of ham (or turkey/chicken), and another slice of Swiss cheese.
   - Top with the remaining bread slices to form sandwiches.
2. **Prepare Egg Batter:**
   - In a shallow dish or pie plate, whisk together eggs, milk, salt, and pepper until well combined.
3. **Dip Sandwiches:**
   - Dip each sandwich into the egg batter, coating both sides evenly. Allow excess batter to drip off.
4. **Cook the Sandwiches:**
   - Heat a large skillet or griddle over medium heat. Add a tablespoon of butter or oil.
   - Place the dipped sandwiches in the skillet and cook for 3-4 minutes on each side, or until golden brown and the cheese is melted.
   - If necessary, press down gently with a spatula to flatten the sandwiches slightly and ensure even cooking.
5. **Serve:**
   - Remove the Monte Cristo sandwiches from the skillet and let them cool slightly on a cutting board.
   - Optionally, dust with powdered sugar.
   - Cut each sandwich diagonally and serve warm.
   - Serve with maple syrup or jam on the side for dipping, if desired.

Monte Cristo sandwiches are a delicious blend of savory and sweet flavors, making them a popular choice for brunch or a special lunch. They are versatile, so feel free to adjust the ingredients to suit your taste preferences. Enjoy this indulgent treat!

Cranberry Scones

Ingredients:

- 2 cups all-purpose flour
- 1/4 cup granulated sugar
- 1 tablespoon baking powder
- 1/2 teaspoon salt
- 1/2 cup unsalted butter, cold and cut into small cubes
- 1/2 cup dried cranberries (or fresh cranberries, chopped)
- 2/3 cup heavy cream (plus extra for brushing)
- 1 large egg
- 1 teaspoon vanilla extract
- Optional: Coarse sugar for sprinkling on top

Instructions:

1. **Preheat Oven:**
   - Preheat your oven to 400°F (200°C). Line a baking sheet with parchment paper or silicone mat.
2. **Mix Dry Ingredients:**
   - In a large bowl, whisk together the flour, sugar, baking powder, and salt.
3. **Add Butter:**
   - Add the cold butter cubes to the flour mixture. Use a pastry cutter, two knives, or your fingertips to quickly cut the butter into the flour until the mixture resembles coarse crumbs. Some larger pea-sized pieces of butter are okay.
4. **Add Cranberries:**
   - Stir in the dried cranberries until evenly distributed throughout the mixture.
5. **Combine Wet Ingredients:**
   - In a separate bowl, whisk together the heavy cream, egg, and vanilla extract until well combined.
6. **Form Dough:**
   - Make a well in the center of the dry ingredients and pour in the wet ingredients. Stir with a wooden spoon or rubber spatula until the dough just starts to come together. It will be slightly sticky.
7. **Shape Scones:**
   - Transfer the dough onto a lightly floured surface. Gently knead the dough a few times until it holds together. Pat the dough into a circle about 1 inch thick.
8. **Cut Scones:**
   - Use a sharp knife or a bench scraper to cut the dough into 8 wedges (like a pizza). Alternatively, you can use a round cutter for traditional round scones.
9. **Bake:**
   - Place the scones onto the prepared baking sheet, spacing them a few inches apart.

- Brush the tops of the scones with a little heavy cream and sprinkle with coarse sugar if desired.
- Bake for 15-18 minutes, or until the scones are golden brown on top and cooked through.

10. **Cool and Serve:**
    - Remove the scones from the oven and let them cool on the baking sheet for a few minutes before transferring to a wire rack to cool completely.
    - Serve the cranberry scones warm or at room temperature. Enjoy with clotted cream, butter, or your favorite jam.

These cranberry scones are best enjoyed fresh on the day they are made, but you can store them in an airtight container at room temperature for up to 2 days. They can also be frozen for longer storage; just thaw and reheat before serving. Enjoy your homemade cranberry scones as a delicious treat!

Breakfast Quinoa

Ingredients:

- 1 cup quinoa, rinsed
- 2 cups water or milk (dairy or plant-based)
- 1 tablespoon honey or maple syrup (optional)
- 1/2 teaspoon vanilla extract
- 1/2 teaspoon ground cinnamon
- Pinch of salt
- Toppings of your choice, such as fresh fruit (berries, sliced bananas), nuts (almonds, walnuts), seeds (chia seeds, flaxseeds), dried fruit (cranberries, raisins), yogurt, or coconut flakes

Instructions:

1. **Rinse Quinoa:**
   - Rinse the quinoa under cold water in a fine-mesh sieve to remove any bitterness.
2. **Cook Quinoa:**
   - In a medium saucepan, combine the rinsed quinoa with water or milk. Bring to a boil over medium-high heat.
   - Reduce the heat to low, cover the saucepan, and simmer for 15-20 minutes, or until the quinoa is cooked and the liquid is absorbed. The quinoa should be tender but still have a slight bite to it.
3. **Flavor Quinoa:**
   - Once the quinoa is cooked, remove from heat. Stir in honey or maple syrup (if using), vanilla extract, ground cinnamon, and a pinch of salt. Adjust sweetness and cinnamon to taste.
4. **Serve:**
   - Divide the breakfast quinoa into bowls. Top with your choice of toppings, such as fresh fruit, nuts, seeds, dried fruit, yogurt, or coconut flakes.
5. **Enjoy:**
   - Serve the breakfast quinoa warm and enjoy it as a nutritious and satisfying breakfast.

Variations:

- **Chocolate Quinoa:** Stir in cocoa powder and a little bit of sweetener (honey or maple syrup) to the cooked quinoa.
- **Savory Quinoa:** Skip the sweeteners and cinnamon, and instead add sautéed vegetables, cooked chicken or tofu, and a drizzle of soy sauce for a savory breakfast option.
- **Pumpkin Spice Quinoa:** Add pumpkin puree, pumpkin pie spice, and a sweetener of your choice to the cooked quinoa for a fall-inspired breakfast.

Breakfast quinoa is versatile and can be customized based on your preferences and dietary needs. It's a great way to incorporate whole grains and protein into your morning routine while enjoying a delicious and filling meal.

Cheddar Bacon Biscuits

Ingredients:

- 2 cups all-purpose flour
- 1 tablespoon baking powder
- 1/2 teaspoon baking soda
- 1/2 teaspoon salt
- 1/2 cup cold unsalted butter, cut into small cubes
- 1 cup shredded cheddar cheese
- 1/2 cup cooked bacon, crumbled (about 6 slices)
- 3/4 cup buttermilk
- Optional: 1-2 tablespoons chopped chives or green onions (for extra flavor)

Instructions:

1. **Preheat Oven:**
   - Preheat your oven to 425°F (220°C). Line a baking sheet with parchment paper or silicone baking mat.
2. **Mix Dry Ingredients:**
   - In a large bowl, whisk together the flour, baking powder, baking soda, and salt.
3. **Cut in Butter:**
   - Add the cold butter cubes to the flour mixture. Use a pastry cutter, two knives, or your fingertips to quickly cut the butter into the flour until the mixture resembles coarse crumbs. Some larger pea-sized pieces of butter are okay.
4. **Add Cheese and Bacon:**
   - Stir in the shredded cheddar cheese and crumbled bacon until evenly distributed throughout the mixture. If using chopped chives or green onions, add them now.
5. **Add Buttermilk:**
   - Make a well in the center of the mixture and pour in the buttermilk. Stir with a wooden spoon or rubber spatula until the dough starts to come together. It will be slightly sticky.
6. **Form Biscuits:**
   - Turn the dough out onto a lightly floured surface. Gently knead the dough a few times until it holds together.
7. **Cut Biscuits:**
   - Pat the dough into a circle or rectangle about 1 inch thick. Use a biscuit cutter or a sharp knife to cut out biscuits. Gather and reroll the scraps as needed to make more biscuits.
8. **Bake:**
   - Place the biscuits on the prepared baking sheet, spacing them about 1 inch apart.
   - Bake for 12-15 minutes, or until the biscuits are golden brown on top and cooked through.
9. **Serve:**

- Remove from the oven and let the biscuits cool on the baking sheet for a few minutes before transferring to a wire rack to cool completely.
- Serve the cheddar bacon biscuits warm. Enjoy them on their own or with butter and your favorite breakfast spread.

These cheddar bacon biscuits are perfect for breakfast or brunch, and they also make a great side dish for soups and salads. They are best enjoyed fresh on the day they are made, but you can store leftovers in an airtight container at room temperature for up to 2 days. Reheat briefly in the oven or microwave before serving. Enjoy your homemade biscuits!

Smoked Salmon Bagel Sandwich

Ingredients:

- 2 bagels, split and toasted (your choice of flavor, such as plain, sesame, or everything)
- 4 ounces smoked salmon, thinly sliced
- 4 tablespoons cream cheese (plain or flavored, such as chive or dill)
- 1/4 red onion, thinly sliced
- 1/2 cucumber, thinly sliced
- Capers, for garnish
- Fresh dill or chives, chopped, for garnish
- Lemon wedges, for serving (optional)
- Salt and pepper, to taste

Instructions:

1. **Toast the Bagels:**
    - Split the bagels and toast them until golden brown. You can toast them in a toaster or under the broiler.
2. **Prepare the Ingredients:**
    - Thinly slice the red onion and cucumber.
    - Chop fresh dill or chives for garnish.
    - Slice the smoked salmon into thin pieces if it's not pre-sliced.
3. **Assemble the Sandwiches:**
    - Spread a generous amount of cream cheese on each toasted bagel half.
    - Layer the smoked salmon slices on the bottom half of each bagel.
    - Top with slices of red onion and cucumber.
4. **Garnish:**
    - Sprinkle capers over the top of each sandwich for added flavor.
    - Garnish with chopped fresh dill or chives.
5. **Season and Serve:**
    - Season with salt and pepper to taste.
    - Serve the smoked salmon bagel sandwiches immediately, optionally with lemon wedges on the side for squeezing over the sandwich.

Variations:

- **Avocado:** Add slices of ripe avocado for extra creaminess and flavor.
- **Tomato:** Include thin slices of ripe tomato for a burst of freshness.
- **Egg:** Add a poached or fried egg to make it more substantial and brunch-worthy.
- **Arugula:** Replace or add arugula for a peppery bite.

Smoked salmon bagel sandwiches are versatile and can be customized based on your preferences. They are perfect for a leisurely weekend breakfast or brunch, or as a quick and satisfying lunch option. Enjoy the rich flavors and textures of this classic sandwich!

Breakfast Enchiladas

Ingredients:

- 8-10 small flour tortillas (8-inch size)
- 8 large eggs
- 1/2 cup milk
- Salt and pepper, to taste
- 1 tablespoon butter or oil
- 1/2 pound breakfast sausage, cooked and crumbled
- 1 cup shredded cheddar cheese, divided
- 1 cup shredded Monterey Jack cheese, divided
- 1 can (10 ounces) red enchilada sauce
- Optional toppings: Chopped cilantro, diced avocado, sour cream, salsa

Instructions:

1. **Preheat Oven:**
   - Preheat your oven to 375°F (190°C). Lightly grease a 9x13-inch baking dish with butter or oil.
2. **Cook Eggs:**
   - In a bowl, whisk together the eggs, milk, salt, and pepper until well combined.
   - Heat butter or oil in a large skillet over medium heat. Pour in the egg mixture and cook, stirring occasionally, until the eggs are scrambled and just set. Remove from heat.
3. **Assemble Enchiladas:**
   - Warm the flour tortillas slightly to make them pliable (you can do this in the microwave or on a dry skillet).
   - Spread about 1/4 cup of enchilada sauce on the bottom of the prepared baking dish.
   - Fill each tortilla with a portion of the scrambled eggs, cooked sausage, and a mixture of shredded cheddar and Monterey Jack cheese. Roll up each tortilla and place seam-side down in the baking dish.
4. **Top with Sauce and Cheese:**
   - Pour the remaining enchilada sauce evenly over the rolled tortillas in the baking dish.
   - Sprinkle the remaining shredded cheese on top of the enchiladas.
5. **Bake:**
   - Cover the baking dish with aluminum foil and bake in the preheated oven for 20 minutes.
   - Remove the foil and bake for an additional 10-15 minutes, or until the cheese is melted and bubbly.
6. **Serve:**
   - Remove from the oven and let the enchiladas cool for a few minutes before serving.

- Garnish with chopped cilantro, diced avocado, sour cream, and salsa as desired.
- Serve warm and enjoy these delicious breakfast enchiladas!

Variations:

- **Vegetarian Option:** Substitute the sausage with sautéed vegetables such as bell peppers, onions, and spinach.
- **Add Beans:** Include refried beans or black beans for extra protein and fiber.
- **Spicy Kick:** Add diced green chilies or jalapeños to the filling for a spicy twist.

Breakfast enchiladas are a filling and flavorful dish that's perfect for feeding a crowd or enjoying as a special weekend breakfast. They can be prepared ahead of time and reheated for a quick and satisfying meal. Customize them with your favorite ingredients and toppings for a delicious breakfast treat!

Spinach and Feta Quiche

Ingredients:

- 1 pre-made pie crust (store-bought or homemade)
- 1 tablespoon olive oil
- 1 small onion, finely chopped
- 2 cloves garlic, minced
- 5 cups fresh spinach leaves, chopped
- 4 large eggs
- 1 cup milk (whole milk or any milk of your choice)
- 1/2 cup crumbled feta cheese
- 1/2 cup shredded mozzarella cheese (optional, for added creaminess)
- 1/4 cup grated Parmesan cheese
- 1/2 teaspoon salt, or to taste
- 1/4 teaspoon black pepper
- Pinch of nutmeg (optional, for added flavor)

Instructions:

1. **Preheat Oven:**
   - Preheat your oven to 375°F (190°C). Place the pie crust in a 9-inch pie dish or quiche pan, pressing it firmly against the bottom and sides. Trim any excess crust if necessary.
2. **Prepare Spinach Mixture:**
   - Heat olive oil in a large skillet over medium heat. Add chopped onion and cook until softened, about 5 minutes.
   - Add minced garlic and cook for another 1-2 minutes until fragrant.
   - Stir in chopped spinach and cook until wilted and any excess moisture has evaporated, about 3-4 minutes. Remove from heat and let cool slightly.
3. **Prepare Egg Mixture:**
   - In a large bowl, whisk together eggs, milk, salt, pepper, and nutmeg (if using) until well combined.
4. **Assemble Quiche:**
   - Spread the spinach mixture evenly over the bottom of the pie crust.
   - Sprinkle crumbled feta cheese, shredded mozzarella cheese (if using), and grated Parmesan cheese over the spinach.
5. **Pour Egg Mixture:**
   - Carefully pour the egg mixture over the spinach and cheese in the pie crust.
6. **Bake:**
   - Place the quiche in the preheated oven and bake for 35-40 minutes, or until the top is golden brown and the center is set. To check for doneness, insert a knife into the center of the quiche; it should come out clean.
7. **Cool and Serve:**

- Remove the quiche from the oven and let it cool for 10 minutes before slicing and serving.
- Serve warm or at room temperature. Enjoy your spinach and feta quiche as a delicious meal!

Variations:

- **Add Protein:** Mix in cooked and crumbled bacon, sausage, or ham for added protein.
- **Vegetarian Option:** Omit the meat and add more vegetables such as bell peppers, mushrooms, or tomatoes.
- **Crustless Quiche:** Skip the pie crust and bake the filling in a greased pie dish or quiche pan. Reduce baking time slightly as needed.

Spinach and feta quiche can be served on its own or paired with a side salad for a complete meal. It's versatile, allowing you to customize the ingredients based on your preferences. Enjoy this flavorful and nutritious dish!

Nutella Stuffed French Toast

Ingredients:

- 4 slices of bread (thick-sliced, such as brioche, challah, or Texas toast)
- Nutella or any chocolate hazelnut spread
- 2 large eggs
- 1/2 cup milk
- 1/2 teaspoon vanilla extract
- Butter or cooking oil, for frying
- Optional toppings: Powdered sugar, fresh berries, sliced bananas, whipped cream, maple syrup

Instructions:

1. **Prepare the Bread:**
    - Spread Nutella generously on 2 slices of bread, covering the entire surface. Press the remaining 2 slices of bread firmly on top to make sandwiches.
2. **Make the Egg Mixture:**
    - In a shallow bowl or pie plate, whisk together eggs, milk, and vanilla extract until well combined.
3. **Dip and Coat:**
    - Dip each Nutella sandwich into the egg mixture, coating both sides evenly. Allow any excess egg mixture to drip off.
4. **Cook the French Toast:**
    - Heat a large skillet or griddle over medium heat and add a pat of butter or a drizzle of cooking oil.
    - Place the dipped sandwiches on the skillet and cook for 3-4 minutes on each side, or until golden brown and the Nutella is warmed and gooey.
5. **Serve:**
    - Remove the Nutella stuffed French toast from the skillet and place them on a plate.
    - Dust with powdered sugar if desired and serve warm.
    - Optionally, top with fresh berries, sliced bananas, whipped cream, or drizzle with maple syrup for extra sweetness.

Enjoy your Nutella stuffed French toast as a delightful breakfast or brunch treat. It's sure to satisfy any chocolate lover's cravings and is perfect for special occasions or whenever you want to indulge in a delicious morning meal!

Breakfast BLT

Ingredients:

- 4 slices of thick-cut bacon
- 4 slices of sandwich bread (toasted, if desired)
- 1 large tomato, thinly sliced
- 2-4 leaves of lettuce (romaine, iceberg, or your choice)
- 2 large eggs
- Salt and pepper, to taste
- Mayonnaise or aioli, for spreading
- Optional: Sliced avocado, for extra creaminess

Instructions:

1. **Cook the Bacon:**
   - In a skillet over medium heat, cook the bacon slices until crispy. Remove from the skillet and drain on paper towels.
2. **Prepare the Eggs:**
   - In the same skillet, cook the eggs sunny-side up or to your preference. Season with salt and pepper.
3. **Assemble the Sandwich:**
   - Spread mayonnaise or aioli on one side of each slice of bread.
   - Layer the tomato slices, cooked bacon, lettuce leaves, and optional sliced avocado on one slice of bread.
4. **Add the Eggs:**
   - Carefully place the cooked eggs on top of the lettuce.
5. **Complete the Sandwich:**
   - Top with the remaining slice of bread, mayo-side down, to complete the sandwich.
6. **Serve:**
   - Slice the Breakfast BLT in half diagonally, if desired.
   - Serve immediately while warm and enjoy!

Variations:

- **Cheese:** Add a slice of cheddar or Swiss cheese for extra flavor and creaminess.
- **Croissant:** Substitute the sandwich bread with a buttery croissant for a more indulgent option.
- **Spicy Mayo:** Mix mayonnaise with a bit of sriracha or your favorite hot sauce for a spicy kick.
- **Bagel:** Use a toasted bagel instead of sandwich bread for a heartier sandwich.

The Breakfast BLT is a satisfying and flavorful sandwich that combines crispy bacon, fresh vegetables, creamy mayo, and perfectly cooked eggs for a delicious start to your day. It's versatile and can be customized based on your preferences, making it a great choice for breakfast or brunch. Enjoy!

Blueberry Breakfast Cake

Ingredients:

- 1/2 cup unsalted butter, softened
- 1 cup granulated sugar
- 2 large eggs
- 1 teaspoon vanilla extract
- 2 cups all-purpose flour
- 2 teaspoons baking powder
- 1/2 teaspoon salt
- 1/2 cup milk (whole milk or any milk of your choice)
- 2 cups fresh or frozen blueberries (if using frozen, do not thaw)

For topping (optional):

- 2 tablespoons granulated sugar
- 1/2 teaspoon ground cinnamon

Instructions:

1. **Preheat Oven and Prepare Pan:**
   - Preheat your oven to 375°F (190°C). Grease and flour a 9-inch round cake pan or line it with parchment paper for easy removal.
2. **Cream Butter and Sugar:**
   - In a large bowl, cream together the softened butter and sugar until light and fluffy.
3. **Add Eggs and Vanilla:**
   - Beat in the eggs, one at a time, until well combined. Stir in the vanilla extract.
4. **Combine Dry Ingredients:**
   - In a separate bowl, whisk together the flour, baking powder, and salt.
5. **Combine Wet and Dry Ingredients:**
   - Gradually add the dry ingredients to the butter mixture, alternating with the milk, beginning and ending with the flour mixture. Mix until just combined. Do not overmix.
6. **Fold in Blueberries:**
   - Gently fold in the blueberries until evenly distributed throughout the batter. If using frozen blueberries, gently fold them in straight from the freezer to avoid excess bleeding.
7. **Prepare Topping (optional):**
   - In a small bowl, combine the sugar and cinnamon for the topping.
8. **Bake:**
   - Pour the batter into the prepared cake pan and spread it evenly.
   - Sprinkle the cinnamon sugar topping evenly over the batter, if using.
9. **Bake:**

- Bake in the preheated oven for 35-40 minutes, or until a toothpick inserted into the center comes out clean and the top is golden brown.

10. **Cool and Serve:**
    - Allow the cake to cool in the pan for 10 minutes before transferring it to a wire rack to cool completely.
    - Slice and serve the blueberry breakfast cake warm or at room temperature. Enjoy!

This blueberry breakfast cake is perfect on its own, but you can also serve it with a dollop of whipped cream or a scoop of vanilla ice cream for an extra special treat. It's a delicious way to enjoy fresh blueberries and make any morning a little sweeter!

Breakfast Stuffed Peppers

Ingredients:

- 4 large bell peppers (any color), halved and seeds removed
- 8 eggs
- 1/2 cup milk (whole milk or any milk of your choice)
- Salt and pepper, to taste
- 1 cup cooked breakfast sausage (crumbled)
- 1 cup shredded cheddar cheese (or any cheese of your choice)
- 1/2 cup diced onion
- 1/2 cup diced bell peppers (from the tops you removed)
- Optional toppings: Chopped fresh herbs (such as parsley or chives), salsa, avocado slices

Instructions:

1. **Preheat Oven:**
   - Preheat your oven to 375°F (190°C). Grease a baking dish large enough to hold all the stuffed pepper halves.
2. **Prepare Peppers:**
   - Cut the bell peppers in half lengthwise and remove the seeds and membranes. Place the pepper halves in the greased baking dish.
3. **Prepare Filling:**
   - In a large bowl, whisk together the eggs, milk, salt, and pepper until well combined.
4. **Assemble Filling:**
   - Stir in the cooked breakfast sausage, shredded cheese, diced onion, and diced bell peppers until evenly distributed.
5. **Fill Peppers:**
   - Spoon the egg mixture into each pepper half, filling them almost to the top.
6. **Bake:**
   - Cover the baking dish with foil and bake in the preheated oven for 25-30 minutes.
7. **Remove Foil and Finish Baking:**
   - Remove the foil and bake for an additional 10-15 minutes, or until the eggs are fully set and the tops are golden brown.
8. **Serve:**
   - Remove from the oven and let the stuffed peppers cool for a few minutes before serving.
   - Garnish with chopped fresh herbs, salsa, avocado slices, or any other toppings you like.

These breakfast stuffed peppers are versatile and can be customized with your favorite breakfast ingredients. They make a hearty and satisfying meal that's perfect for brunch or a weekend breakfast. Enjoy the savory flavors and nutritious benefits of this delicious dish!

Peanut Butter Banana Smoothie

Ingredients:

- 1 ripe banana, peeled and sliced
- 1 tablespoon creamy peanut butter (unsweetened)
- 1 cup milk (dairy or plant-based)
- 1/2 cup plain Greek yogurt
- 1 tablespoon honey or maple syrup (optional, for added sweetness)
- Ice cubes (optional, for a chilled smoothie)

Instructions:

1. **Blend Ingredients:**
   - In a blender, combine the sliced banana, creamy peanut butter, milk, Greek yogurt, and honey or maple syrup (if using).
2. **Blend Until Smooth:**
   - Blend on high speed until all ingredients are smooth and well combined. If you prefer a thicker smoothie, add more banana or yogurt. If you prefer a thinner consistency, add more milk.
3. **Adjust Sweetness (Optional):**
   - Taste the smoothie and add more honey or maple syrup if you prefer a sweeter taste.
4. **Add Ice (Optional):**
   - If desired, add a handful of ice cubes to the blender and blend until the smoothie reaches your desired consistency and temperature.
5. **Serve:**
   - Pour the Peanut Butter Banana Smoothie into glasses.
6. **Garnish (Optional):**
   - Optionally, garnish with a slice of banana or a sprinkle of crushed peanuts on top.
7. **Enjoy:**
   - Serve immediately and enjoy your delicious and creamy Peanut Butter Banana Smoothie!

Variations:

- **Chocolate Peanut Butter Banana Smoothie:** Add a tablespoon of cocoa powder or chocolate protein powder for a chocolatey twist.
- **Green Peanut Butter Banana Smoothie:** Add a handful of spinach or kale for added nutrition (you won't taste the greens!).
- **Nut-Free Option:** Substitute almond butter or sunflower seed butter for peanut butter if you have nut allergies.
- **Protein Boost:** Add a scoop of vanilla or chocolate protein powder for an extra protein kick.

This Peanut Butter Banana Smoothie is a great option for breakfast or as a post-workout snack, providing a good balance of protein, healthy fats, and carbohydrates. It's creamy, satisfying, and sure to become a favorite!

Strawberry Shortcake Pancakes

Ingredients:

For the Pancakes:

- 1 cup all-purpose flour
- 2 tablespoons granulated sugar
- 1 teaspoon baking powder
- 1/2 teaspoon baking soda
- 1/4 teaspoon salt
- 1 cup buttermilk
- 1 large egg
- 2 tablespoons unsalted butter, melted
- 1 teaspoon vanilla extract

For the Strawberry Topping:

- 2 cups fresh strawberries, hulled and sliced
- 2 tablespoons granulated sugar
- Whipped cream, for serving
- Additional sliced strawberries, for garnish (optional)

Instructions:

1. **Prepare the Strawberry Topping:**
   - In a bowl, combine the sliced strawberries with 2 tablespoons of sugar. Stir well until the strawberries are coated. Set aside to macerate while you prepare the pancakes.
2. **Make the Pancake Batter:**
   - In a large bowl, whisk together the flour, sugar, baking powder, baking soda, and salt.
   - In another bowl, whisk together the buttermilk, egg, melted butter, and vanilla extract.
   - Pour the wet ingredients into the dry ingredients and gently stir until just combined. Do not overmix; it's okay if there are some lumps in the batter.
3. **Cook the Pancakes:**
   - Heat a non-stick griddle or skillet over medium heat. Lightly grease the surface with butter or cooking spray.
   - Pour about 1/4 cup of batter onto the griddle for each pancake. Cook until bubbles form on the surface of the pancakes and the edges look set, about 2-3 minutes.
   - Flip the pancakes and cook for another 1-2 minutes, or until golden brown and cooked through.

- Transfer the cooked pancakes to a plate and cover with aluminum foil to keep warm while you cook the remaining pancakes.
4. **Assemble the Strawberry Shortcake Pancakes:**
    - To serve, stack the pancakes on a plate.
    - Top each pancake with a spoonful of the macerated strawberries and their juices.
    - Add a dollop of whipped cream on top of each pancake.
    - Optionally, garnish with additional sliced strawberries for extra freshness.
5. **Serve:**
    - Serve the strawberry shortcake pancakes immediately while warm.
    - Enjoy these delicious pancakes as a special breakfast or brunch treat!

Variations:

- **Add Lemon Zest:** For a hint of citrus flavor, add 1 teaspoon of lemon zest to the pancake batter.
- **Use Different Berries:** Replace strawberries with other berries such as raspberries or blueberries for a different twist.
- **Maple Syrup:** Drizzle with maple syrup instead of whipped cream for a classic pancake topping.

These strawberry shortcake pancakes are fluffy, fruity, and perfect for celebrating a special occasion or treating yourself to a delightful breakfast. Enjoy!

Southwest Breakfast Casserole

Ingredients:

- 1 tablespoon olive oil
- 1 small onion, diced
- 1 red bell pepper, diced
- 1 green bell pepper, diced
- 1 jalapeño pepper, seeded and diced (optional, for heat)
- 1 cup corn kernels (fresh or frozen)
- 1 can (15 ounces) black beans, drained and rinsed
- 1 cup diced cooked ham or cooked breakfast sausage (optional)
- 8 large eggs
- 1/2 cup milk (whole milk or any milk of your choice)
- 1 teaspoon ground cumin
- 1 teaspoon chili powder
- Salt and pepper, to taste
- 1 cup shredded cheddar cheese (or any cheese of your choice)
- Optional toppings: Chopped fresh cilantro, salsa, sour cream, avocado slices

Instructions:

1. **Preheat Oven:**
    - Preheat your oven to 375°F (190°C). Grease a 9x13-inch baking dish with cooking spray or butter.
2. **Cook Vegetables:**
    - In a large skillet, heat olive oil over medium heat. Add diced onion, red bell pepper, green bell pepper, and jalapeño pepper (if using). Cook until softened, about 5-7 minutes.
    - Stir in corn kernels and cook for an additional 2-3 minutes. Remove from heat and let cool slightly.
3. **Prepare Casserole:**
    - In a large bowl, whisk together eggs, milk, ground cumin, chili powder, salt, and pepper.
4. **Combine Ingredients:**
    - Add the cooked vegetables, black beans, diced ham or sausage (if using), and half of the shredded cheese to the egg mixture. Stir until well combined.
5. **Assemble and Bake:**
    - Pour the egg mixture into the prepared baking dish, spreading it evenly.
    - Sprinkle the remaining shredded cheese on top of the casserole.
6. **Bake:**
    - Bake in the preheated oven for 25-30 minutes, or until the casserole is set in the center and the cheese is melted and bubbly.
7. **Serve:**

- Remove from the oven and let the casserole cool for a few minutes before slicing.
- Garnish with chopped fresh cilantro, salsa, sour cream, and avocado slices if desired.
- Serve warm and enjoy this flavorful Southwest breakfast casserole!

Variations:

- **Vegetarian Option:** Omit the ham or sausage and add more vegetables like mushrooms or spinach.
- **Spicy Kick:** Add diced green chilies or extra jalapeños for a spicier version.
- **Cheese:** Experiment with different cheeses such as pepper jack or Monterey Jack for added flavor.
- **Tortilla Chips:** Layer crushed tortilla chips on top before baking for a crunchy texture.

This Southwest breakfast casserole is perfect for feeding a crowd or meal prepping for busy mornings. It's versatile and can be customized with your favorite Tex-Mex ingredients. Enjoy the delicious flavors and hearty satisfaction of this breakfast dish!

Pecan Sticky Buns

Ingredients:

For the Dough:

- 3 1/2 cups all-purpose flour
- 1/4 cup granulated sugar
- 1 teaspoon salt
- 2 1/4 teaspoons (1 packet) instant yeast
- 1 cup milk, warmed to about 110°F (43°C)
- 1/4 cup unsalted butter, melted
- 1 large egg

For the Filling:

- 1/2 cup unsalted butter, softened
- 1 cup packed brown sugar
- 1 tablespoon ground cinnamon
- 1/2 cup chopped pecans

For the Sticky Caramel Topping:

- 1/2 cup unsalted butter
- 1 cup packed brown sugar
- 1/2 cup heavy cream
- 1/2 cup light corn syrup
- 1 teaspoon vanilla extract
- 1 cup chopped pecans

Instructions:

1. **Make the Dough:**
    - In a large mixing bowl, combine 3 cups of flour, granulated sugar, salt, and yeast.
    - In a separate bowl, whisk together warm milk, melted butter, and egg.
    - Pour the wet ingredients into the dry ingredients and mix until a dough forms.
    - Gradually add the remaining 1/2 cup of flour, kneading until the dough is smooth and elastic, about 5-7 minutes.
    - Place the dough in a greased bowl, cover with plastic wrap or a clean kitchen towel, and let it rise in a warm place until doubled in size, about 1-2 hours.
2. **Prepare the Caramel Topping:**
    - In a medium saucepan, melt butter over medium heat.
    - Stir in brown sugar, heavy cream, and corn syrup. Cook, stirring constantly, until sugar is dissolved and mixture is smooth.
    - Remove from heat and stir in vanilla extract. Let cool slightly.
3. **Assemble the Sticky Buns:**

- Grease a 9x13-inch baking dish and spread the cooled caramel topping evenly over the bottom.
- Sprinkle chopped pecans over the caramel topping.

4. **Roll and Fill the Dough:**
    - Punch down the risen dough and roll it out on a lightly floured surface into a rectangle about 12x18 inches.
    - Spread softened butter evenly over the dough.
    - In a small bowl, mix together brown sugar and cinnamon. Sprinkle the mixture evenly over the buttered dough, then sprinkle with chopped pecans.

5. **Roll and Cut the Buns:**
    - Starting from the long edge, tightly roll up the dough into a log.
    - Cut the log into 12 equal slices using a sharp knife or dental floss for clean cuts.
    - Place the slices cut-side down in the prepared baking dish on top of the caramel topping and pecans.

6. **Final Rise and Bake:**
    - Cover the baking dish with plastic wrap and let the buns rise in a warm place until doubled in size, about 30-45 minutes.
    - Preheat your oven to 350°F (175°C).
    - Bake the sticky buns in the preheated oven for 25-30 minutes, or until golden brown and bubbling.

7. **Cool and Serve:**
    - Remove the sticky buns from the oven and let them cool in the baking dish for 5-10 minutes.
    - Carefully invert the sticky buns onto a serving platter or baking sheet so that the caramel pecan topping is on top.
    - Serve warm and enjoy the decadent pecan sticky buns!

These pecan sticky buns are best served warm, allowing the caramel topping to remain gooey and the pecans crunchy. They are perfect for a special breakfast or brunch treat that will impress your family and friends!

Chocolate Chip Pancakes

Ingredients:

- 1 cup all-purpose flour
- 1 tablespoon granulated sugar
- 1 teaspoon baking powder
- 1/2 teaspoon baking soda
- 1/4 teaspoon salt
- 1 cup buttermilk
- 1 large egg
- 2 tablespoons unsalted butter, melted
- 1 teaspoon vanilla extract
- 1/2 cup chocolate chips (semi-sweet or milk chocolate)

Instructions:

1. **Prepare the Batter:**
   - In a large bowl, whisk together the flour, sugar, baking powder, baking soda, and salt.
2. **Mix Wet Ingredients:**
   - In another bowl, whisk together the buttermilk, egg, melted butter, and vanilla extract until well combined.
3. **Combine Wet and Dry Ingredients:**
   - Pour the wet ingredients into the dry ingredients and stir until just combined. Be careful not to overmix; it's okay if there are a few lumps.
4. **Add Chocolate Chips:**
   - Gently fold in the chocolate chips into the pancake batter.
5. **Cook the Pancakes:**
   - Heat a non-stick skillet or griddle over medium heat. Lightly grease the surface with butter or cooking spray.
   - Pour about 1/4 cup of batter onto the skillet for each pancake. Spread the batter slightly with the back of a spoon if needed.
   - Cook until bubbles form on the surface of the pancakes and the edges look set, about 2-3 minutes.
6. **Flip and Cook:**
   - Flip the pancakes and cook for another 1-2 minutes, or until golden brown and cooked through.
7. **Serve:**
   - Stack the chocolate chip pancakes on a plate.
   - Optionally, top with additional chocolate chips, maple syrup, whipped cream, or sliced bananas.
8. **Enjoy:**
   - Serve warm and enjoy these delicious chocolate chip pancakes as a special breakfast treat!

Variations:

- **Banana Chocolate Chip Pancakes:** Add mashed ripe banana to the batter for extra flavor and sweetness.
- **Double Chocolate Chip Pancakes:** Use chocolate pancake mix or add cocoa powder to the batter for a richer chocolate flavor.
- **Nutty Twist:** Add chopped nuts such as walnuts or pecans along with the chocolate chips for added texture.
- **Fruity Delight:** Serve with fresh berries or sliced strawberries on top for a burst of freshness.

These chocolate chip pancakes are sure to be a hit with chocolate lovers of all ages. They are fluffy, indulgent, and perfect for weekend mornings or special occasions. Enjoy!